TOMORROW BEGINS
AT 3:00

More Time Management Tips for Teachers

BY SCOTT PURDY

Also by Scott Purdy

Time Management for Teachers
Teaching Students to Write
The Write Time Teacher Planbook
A Hands On Approach to Teaching Statistics, Probability, and Graphing
A Hands On Approach to Teaching Measurement
A Hands On Approach to Teaching Logic
A Hands On Approach to Teaching Geometry
A Hands On Approach to Teaching Algebra
A Hands On Approach to Teaching Patterns and Functions
A Hands On Approach to Teaching Number and Operations

For information, please contact
WRITE TIME PUBLISHING
2121 Rebild Dr.   Solvang, California 93463-2217
(800) 824-3376
FAX: (805) 688-7802
online: www.writetimepub.com

Table of Contents

Introduction

Six years ago, when I began writing my first book, <u>Time Management for Teachers</u>, there was a nagging question. I kept wondering, "Do I really have enough to say to fill a book?" I knew that substitute teachers, classroom management, grading papers, discipline, and applying technology were issues that teachers had to cope with on a consistent basis. As it turned out, filling the first book with practical tips to aid in these areas was not a problem. The difficulty was in attaining my goal of presenting these ideas in a text that a person could read in two to three hours.

Now, I enter round two in my attempt to make teaching more manageable, rewarding, and interesting. You are holding the result of this effort, <u>Tomorrow Begins at 3:00</u>.

In this book, I share some of the more specific ideas and approaches that have allowed me to continue to teach (my first love) while presenting twenty to thirty district inservices and twenty-five college level week-end seminars each year. In addition to my teaching duties, I do all the bookkeeping, shipping, and advertising for a series of seven math books I co-

authored with fellow teachers and perform the same managerial functions for my own company, Write Time Publishing. Over the past six months, I have finished my first book on teaching writing and have designed and published a teacher planner.

Add to all of this that I have been happily married for thirty years, have three children who have graduated from or are attending college, spend my summers at a home I built in Colorado, and one can see that I do believe that teachers can have it all!

Time management and personal organization have opened many doors for me. It has had the same impact upon hundreds of teachers who have attended my seminars and read my first book.

One of the "doors" I chose to access was entrepreneurial; the opportunities that fellow teachers have chosen have varied. For some, it was to have more time to read, for others, it was time to spend with their children or spouse. I know of several teachers who now spend their entire summer traveling. They finance these excursions with money earned by completing the ten salary units I encourage teachers to take each school year.

Time management allows each individual to take control of his or her professional life and re-establish priorities in one's personal life.

One might think that with the topics already discussed in a previous book, what is left? In this text, I will present some very unique ideas for teachers of every grade level and every subject area. I begin with a chapter on year-long planning. It is one of the most significant time-savers a teacher can implement.

The second chapter discusses a concept I refer to as "Universal Homework." The idea here is that students need not be in class on any particular day in order to complete that night's homework assignment. It, too, is a dramatic time saver.

Chapter three extends and completes the presentation of the year-long plan. It presents the practical application of blending long-range planning and universal homework.

Chapter four is dedicated to the opening of school. It is the most important time of the year. It is when you train your students, and more importantly, you enlist the support of the parents of your students. If you are going to complete your planning and correcting for the following day between 3:00 and 4:00 and walk out of your classroom everyday at 4:00, you must implement an organized structure that those around you support. The time to establish your procedures is at the beginning of the school year.

The fifth chapter is quite lengthy and presents twenty-five new time-saving ideas I have developed over the past five years. While each teacher will not use all twenty-five, I believe every teacher will find several of the techniques are applicable for his or her teaching situation.

The book closes with a chapter focusing on the "Professional Teacher." I learned many years ago that the more I assume a stance of a professional, the more professionally I am treated by everyone with whom I come in contact. In this chapter, I present several ideas that you can use to assume a new status as a professional.

A brief comment about the title... I was driving to Los Angeles one morning last year to present a seminar, and the title, "Tomorrow Begins at 3:00," popped into my mind. To me it represents the fundamental concept of time manage-

ment. It is not a matter of wishing one's life away, it is a matter of taking control and knowing when the professional ends and the personal begins. Teachers must make the distinction between time on and time off. The job of teaching can fill every waking moment if we let that happen. If we are going to be successful teachers we must be successful in our personal lives as well.

The Year-long Plan
Part One

I ascribe to the philosophy that when you identify a task that you think you can comfortably accomplish in a given amount of time, double the task. For example, if you now plan one teaching day at a time, and if it takes you one hour to prepare, your goal tomorrow should be to prepare lesson plans for two days within that one hour. If you believe you can correct ten math papers in fifteen minutes, make it a goal to correct twenty.

The logic to this approach is that things will take as long as you allow them to take. I use this doubling techinique in almost all aspects of my professional life, and while I do not always accomplish twice as much, I always complete more than I think I can.

Many teachers might look at a chapter on year-long planning and think, "I can't plan for a year!" Yes, you can, and when you do, you will do a better job of teaching than you have ever done before. I also urge you not to give in to the temptation of planning for one third or one half of the year. We can all plan for the year.

Where and when do we begin?

The chances that you happen to be reading this chapter at the beginning of a school year are slim. The approach will work at a variety of times. You can institute the year-long planning concept during any natural break in the year — winter vacation, spring break or at the end of a quarter or semester. The ideal is, of course, prior to the first day of classes. Starting in mid-year does simplify the task and give some good practice for when you tackle your full-year plan for the next school year.

In a year-long plan we are not concerned with details, methodology of instruction, creating lessons and tests, or the other components of the daily planning process. Your objective is to identify how will you fit your required curriculum into a 180 day (typical) school year.

Whether you are a third grade "self-contained" teacher or a high school physics teacher, there is a curriculum which is established for you. Typically, the curriculum is your textbook and has been embellished or refined by a school district curriculum guide.

The high school physics teacher faces the dilemma of how to cover 500 pages of text, divided into eighteen chapters, while assuring that students gain sufficient mastery to successfully pass some type of standardized exam. The limitation is to cover all of this information in 180 class sessions (usually shortened to 170 or fewer by school assemblies, sports events, and teacher inservice days). The added challenge is to also prepare the same year-long plan for a pre-calculus class, an applied physics class, and a beginning level physical science class.

For the elementary teacher, the year-long plan must include six to eight science units ranging from physical to life to earth sciences; a social studies curriculum which covers at least 300 years of history; a reading program which usually involves grouping students and integrates a basal reader and three to six novels; a math curriculum which can also involve grouping and is based upon a hierarchy which includes instruction in four operations, geometry, measurement, logic, and statistics (to mention a few); a writing program in which students learn spelling, punctuation, grammar, paragraph structure, and creativity; and throw into this mix music, art, physical education, health, and computer.

Needless to say, it is remarkable that any teacher is able to teach all that we are asked to teach! It is also not surprising that we often do not complete the entire scope of our curricula.

The demands placed upon an elementary school teacher and a high school teacher are different; however, given the fact that self-contained teachers must plan for every curricular area, I will use the fifth grade as a model as to how to complete a year-long plan.

A Fifth Grade Year-long Plan

There are four steps to completing this plan. First, we list the material to be covered. Second, we graph the information so we can integrate and blend related topics. Third, we organize our writing assignments around the content which we are teaching. Fourth, we create universal assignments to facilitate planning within each subject area.

Step 1: Outlining topics to be covered

We start this process by outlining the units, chapters, and number of pages to be covered within each of the instructional areas.

Fifth Grade Science Text

I. Astronomy (64 pages)
> A. Chapters
>> 1. Movement and Gravity
>> 2. The Planets
>> 3. Earth
>
> B. Vocabulary

biosphere	Earth	hydrosphere
system	atmosphere	interaction
diversity	energy	plankton
lithosphere	meteorites	Mercury
Venus	Mars	rotation
Pluto	Jupiter	Saturn
Neptune	revolution	axis
mass	ellipse	meteor
gravity	solar eclipse	

II. Geology (72 pages)
> A. Chapters
>> 1. Water
>> 2. Erosion
>> 3. Fresh and Salt Water
>
> B. Vocabulary

solution	float	cycle
pollution	mixture	molecule
surface	tension	dissolve
erosion	minerals	glaciers
weathering	oxygen	dark zone
adaptation	pressure	reefs
light zone	adapted	erode

III. Geology (64 pages)

    A. Chapters

        1. Tectonic plates

        2. Volcanoes

        3. Earthquakes

    B. Vocabulary

pressure	plates	lava
core	mantle	magma
Mid-Atlantic	ridge	subduction
crust	volcano	chamber
ash	seismograph	colonizers
granite	earthquake	islands
electricity	survivors	folded
predict	fault	Appalachian
Sierras	plates	slides
Richter Scale	fault-block	volcano
pumice	survivors	

IV. Aeronautics (64 pages)

    A. Chapters

        1. The Earth's Atmosphere

        2. How Bird's Fly

        3. Flight

    B. Vocabulary

air resistance	dense	oxygen
nitrogen	atmosphere	sinks
rises	greater	gravity
air pressure	stratosphere	hollow
adapted	thrust	low pressure
hover	lift	calories
pollution	subsonic	glider
jet propulsion	high pressure	expands
supersonic	sonic boom	flight

V. Meteorology (64 pages)

    A. Chapters

        1. Changing Weather

        2. Climate

        3. Predicting Weather

B. Vocabulary

humidity	saturated air	air mass
front	rotation	water vapor
pressure	atmosphere	condenses
climate	adapted	tropical
seasons	attitude	grassland
deciduous	solstice	temperate
rain gauge	expands	hurricane
meteorologist	computers	precipitation
wind speed	wind vane	barometer

VI. Ecology (64 pages)

A. Chapters

1. Life in the Rainforest
2. The Changing Rainforest
3. Protecting Rainforests

B. Vocabulary

equator	partnerships	decomposers
rainforests	ecosystem	species
pollination	canopy	population
extinct	cycle	prescription
medicines	oxygen	carbon dioxide
greenhouse effect	biosphere	harvested
conservation	recycling	consumer

Each unit is divided into three chapters of approximately eighteen pages. Each of these sub-chapters has an experiment or activity to do in class upon completion. Also, sub-chapters have a set of six to eight **chapter review** questions.

The **unit review** section has an average of five questions which summarize the entire chapter, plus another four questions which allow students to apply the information that has been presented.

You must decide if it is possible to cover the entire book. With thirty-eight weeks in the school year, less one week at

the beginning of and another non-content week at the close, you will need to complete six units in thirty-six weeks. This allows six weeks per unit. Therefore, it is probably possible to cover all of the material.

Fifth Grade Social Studies Text

I. The United States in the Past and Present (79 pages)
   A. Chapters
      1. A Nation of Different People
      2. Our Land
      3. Clues to the Past
   B. Vocabulary

culture	descendent	ethnic
custom	immigrant	pluralism
predjudice	cartographer	fault
geography	hemisphere	latitude
longitude	meridian	parallel
physical map	projection	region
archives	artifact	chronology
empathy	evidence	historian
interpret	journal	oral history
primary source		

II. Exploring and Settling America (75 pages)
   A. Chapters
      1. The First Americans
      2. Exploring America
      3. Settling a New World
   B. Vocabulary

agriculture	confederation	epoch
glacier	long house	mesa
mound	potlatch	colony
contagious	expedition	navigate
technology	colonization	encomienda
fort	investor	Northwest Passage
mission	pacifism	Pilgrim
profit	Puritan	Quaker

11

III. The English Colonies (80 pages)

    A. Chapters

        1. Colonies in the South

        2. Colonies in New England

        3. The Middle Colonies

    B. Vocabulary

cash crop	council	export
plantation	rebel	slavery
apprentice	common	indentured servant
covenant	representative	democracy
dissenter	duty	life expectancy
merchant	Parliament	smuggle
civil disobedience	diversity	landlord
navigable	patroon	system
tolerance	treaty	tenant farmer

IV. Struggling for Independence (80 pages)

    A. Chapters

        1. Struggles with Britain

        2. The Beginnings of War

        3. The Search of Unity

    B. Vocabulary

assembly	boycott	import
politics	propoganda	repeal
veto	civilian	constitution
delagate	equality	independence
Loyalist	militia	republic
revolution	amendment	compromise
federal	ratify	checks and balances
legislature	patriotism	separation of power
township		

V. Life in a New Nation (86 pages)

    A. Chapters

        1. Birth of a Nation

        2. Moving West

        3. Settlements in the West

    B. Vocabulary

Cabinet	camp meeting	common school
Federalist	nationalism	precedent

Monroe Doctrine	impressment	Republican
surplus	textile	political party
War Hawk	canal	ordinance
pioneer	tributary	annex
claim	forty-niner	migrate
Mormon	plain	

VI. America in Conflict (78 pages)

A. Chapters

    1. Life in the South

    2. The North

    3. A Divided Nation

B. Vocabulary

abolitionist	cotton gin	overseer
sharecropper	spiritual	factory
reform	tenement	industrial
Shaker	slum	utopian community
walking city	Confederacy	emancipation
free state	secede	secessionist
slave state	Union	united
Underground Railway		

VII. The Future of America (47 pages)

A. Chapters

    1. Life in a Changing America

    2. The Promise of America

B. Vocabulary

ghetto	labor union	mechanization
middle class	nativism	racism
strike	civil rights	citizenship
discrimination	minority	petition
registration	segregation	self-interest
suffrage		

Again, you must decide if you can cover all units. With thirty-six teaching weeks, it allows five weeks to present each unit. However, considering that there are 520 pages in the text, I do not believe it is realistic to think that all seven units can be covered effectively.

13

These are the types of decisions that should be made before the school year begins. In looking at the seven units, I would omit unit one and unit seven. I would rather have time to adequately cover exploration, colonization, revolution, westward expansion, and the Civil War than to try to start from the beginning of the book and only get to unit five. Being realistic is part of time management.

Fifth Grade Math Text

In workshops, I am surprised by how many teachers do not have math books or have books but do not like or use them. I will assume that you have a book and choose to follow it as your curriculum. My opinion is that if you have a textbook, regardless of its contents, use it as a guide in year-long planning. You need not use it every day, but it undoubtedly has some information that is useful.

The contents of a typical fifth grade text might include:

I. Place Value, Addition, and Subtraction of Whole Numbers
II. Addition and Subtraction of Decimals
III. Multiplication of Whole Numbers
IV. Multiplying Decimals
V. Dividing Whole Numbers and Decimals
VI. Division with Two Digit Divisors
VII. Adding and Subtracting Fractions
VIII. Multiplying and Dividing Fractions
IX. Measurement
X. Ratio and Percent
XI. Geometry
XII. Statistics and Probability

The math series presented here is very traditional in its approach. The chapters progress from addition and subtraction of whole numbers and decimals to multiplication of whole numbers and decimals. There is an emphasis on division in the middle units since this is a definite fifth grade mastery skill. Another chapter presents fractions, and of course, there are the obligatory sections on measurement, geometry, and statistics.

The decision here is not whether the entire curriculum can be covered, it is how a teacher can do as much whole class instruction as possible. This theme will be developed as we continue with the year-long plan.

Fifth Grade Language/Grammar Text

As a middle school writing teacher, I will admit to a strong affinity for teaching grammar. With all that teachers have to do, it is not surprising that some things fall by the wayside. Unfortunately, since grammar is not the most stimulating topic to teach (or to learn), it is often de-emphasized or ignored.

As a component of applying time management into your teaching, note that there is a column dedicated to writing on the chart on pages 20 and 21. The writing component is closely related to the language/grammar program which you present to your students.

Part One

I. Developing paragraphs
    A. Writing the topic sentence
    B. Supporting with details
    C. Placing details in order

C. Telling a story
D. Listening for specifics
E. Listening to poems
F. Extra: compound and hyphenated words

VII. Dictionary Skills

A. Locating words
B. Syllabication and pronunciation
C. Choosing definitions
D. Identifying parts of speech
E. The thesaurus
F. Extra: idiomatic expressions

Part Two

I. Parts of Speech

A. Nouns
B. Pronouns
C. Adjectives
D. Verbs
E. Adverbs
F. Prepositions, Conjunctions, and Interjections
G. Sentence types
H. Punctuation
I. Capitalization

The number of pages per chapter are not included here because typically these concepts are not taught page by page as are social studies or science. Language arts concepts are explained through discussion and examples. Also, exercises are interspersed throughout the text so there is little comparison to the content areas.

It is safe to assume that in the fifth grade, students will probably learn dictionary skills, letter writing, creative story writing, prepare at least one oral presentation, write a report of some kind, discuss grammar, and learn about punctuation.

Given this, the content of the language book will be covered. The year-long plan simply provides a commitment to present all of this information.

Reading and Literature

It is almost impossible to generalize an approach to teaching reading. There are literature-based approaches, team teaching concepts, basal readers, novel centered instruction, thematic reading units, and a myriad of other models. Additionally, there is usually more grouping done for reading instruction than any other subject area.

All of this makes it difficult to include reading in the chart in this sample year-long plan. There are two approaches one can take.

First, since reading instruction is a daily event in almost every classroom, it can be completely separated from the integration of the other subject areas. This decision is made easier when the writing and language programs are linked closely with content areas of social studies and science. Reading can be taught as a unit unto itself. This approach is very effective.

Second, novels and literary genre can be closely linked to the science, social studies, language, and writing curricula. This is the approach outlined in the year-long chart on pages 20 and 21.

Step 2: Coordinating units on a year-long grid

With the subject area outlines complete, and some basic decisions as to what will be included and what will be omitted from the texts, we now place this information on a grid or

chart. Pages 21 and 22 give an example of how a year-long plan might look.

Step 3: Creating the writing component of the year-long plan

There are a number of subtle changes in the order of instruction and numerous entries that need explanation. Most of these concern the writing assignments that integrate and expand the year-long curriculum. These notes are cross referenced by the ① through ⑬ numbers on the chart.

① The first two writing assignments are an autobiography and biography. The autobiography is an appropriate way to start the year in that you can learn a lot about your students' personal lives as well as their writing skills.

The biography of a parent or grandparent is a link to the first social studies units — Exploration and Settlement of America. Obviously, the grandparents of your students did not arrive on the Mayflower; however, many did come as immigrants or were second generation Americans. The multicultural aspect is that in America, we are all foreigners.

② The first novel read by the the entire class is a fantasy. Since the science unit is the solar system, The Lion, the Witch, and the Wardrobe provides an interesting connection. This also sets the stage for the next two writing assignments.

③ The third writing assignment allows students to write their first story. Since they will have already read a portion of the science fiction novel, this can be used a model for the story.

	Language Arts	Science	Social Studies	Math	Writing
Week 1	Developing paragraphs &			Unit 1 Place Value,	Autobiography ①
Week 2	Nouns.pronouns	Solar System	Unit 2 Exploration and Settlement of America	Addition & Subtraction of Whole Numbers	Biography
Week 3	Novel: The Lion, the Witch, and the Wardrobe				Parent or Grandparent
Week 4				Unit 2 Addition & Subtraction of Decimals	
Week 5	②				Space Travel Story
Week 6	Improving your writing &				③
Week 7	Adjectives &	Science Test Week		Unit 3 Multiplying Whole Numbers	Book Report Science Fiction
Week 8	Capitalization	Water Cycle & Oceans	Social Studies Test Week		
Week 9	Novel: I, Columbus		Unit 3		
		Report Cards			
Week 10			The Colonies	Unit 4 Multiplying Decimals	A Day in the Life of a Sea Animal
Week 11	Dictionary Skills &				④
Week 12	Verbs				A Day in the Life of a Colonist
Week 13		Science Test Week		Unit9 Geometry	
Week 14		Volcanoes & Earthquakes		⑤	Book Report
Week 15			Social Studies Test Week		⑥
Week 16			Unit 4		A Legend
		Winter Vacation			
Week 17	New writing ideas &		Independence & Revolution	Unit 5 Dividing	Explaining Natural Phenomenon
Week 18	Adverbs Novel: The Winter of Red Snow			Whole Numbers &	Descriptive Essay American Location
Week 19		Science Test Week		Decimals	
		Report Cards			

	Language Arts	Science	Social Studies	Math	Writing
Week 20		Aeronautics		Unit 6 Division	Fighting for a Cause
Week 21				Two Digit Divisors	(7)
Week 22	Writing reports		Social Studies Test Week		Book report
Week 23			Unit 5 Westward Expansion	Unit 9 Measurement	(8)
Week 24					Report on a person
Week 25		Science Test Week		(9)	
Week 26		Weather		Unit 8 Adding & Subtracting Fractions	Letter writing: Business letter to a company
Week 27	Letter writing & Prepositions,				
Week 28			Social Studies Test Week		(10)
Report Cards/Spring Vacation					
Week 29	Conjunctions, and Interjections		Unit 6 The Civil War	Unit 8 Multiplying & Dividing Fractions	Letter writing: A letter home from the West
Week 30	Novel: Across Five Aprils				
Week 31		Science Test Week			Book Report
Week 32	Speaking Skills &	Rainforests & Ecology		Unit 10 Ratio & Percent	(12)
Week 33				(11)	Comparison Contrast North vs. South
Week 34					
Week 35				Unit 12 Statistics & Probability	Alone Essay Alone in nature
Week 36					(13)
Week 37		Science Test Week	Social Studies Test Week		Oral Reports Alone in nature
Week 38					
Report Cards					

The book report format for the fourth writing assignment can be drawn from the suggestions given on page 42.

④ As report card and parent conference time arrives, the second science and social studies units, and another novel become the new curricular areas. The suggested writing assignments for this month epitomize the philosphy of "two-fer" planning.

This concept is identified several times in future chapters. Basically, it means that whenever you plan one lesson, try to use the same format or plan for a second lesson. The writing assignments focus on the idea of "a day in the life." Both require the students to use their imaginations, but both are based upon the factual information presented in the science unit on oceanography and the social studies unit describing Colonial America.

When students do two consecutive writing assignments, it eliminates the need for them to do rewrites of either. They can apply the teacher's suggestions from the first essay as they write their second. They can also use some of the same approaches and paragraph structure so less time need be spent by the teacher in explaining the assignment.

Consecutive, similar assignments cannot be given month after month, but two or three of these "sets" is a very clever way to simplify planning while giving students a unique way to apply what they have learned.

⑤ Of all the topics we teach, math is the most challenging to keep on schedule. The skills in math are so measurable and sequential that when students do not master a specific concept, there is no way to keep pushing forward. The teacher must stop and assure mastery.

However, I also believe any teacher at any grade level can begin the year with whole group instruction for the first three chapters of the math book. Automatically making a decision to assign a student to a low group based upon the impression of the previous year's teacher or upon a standardized test score is a mistake.

As the year progresses, most teachers are forced to divide the class into groups to allow some to move ahead to new curriculum while others review unmastered skills. This ebb and flow of groupings is an essential component to keep in mind when planning for the year.

Rather than split the class into groups for the remainder of the year, this year-long plan will enable the teacher to divide the class into two groups until winter vacation. To accomplish this, I would rearrange the order of presentation of the chapters. The geometry unit would be taught in its entirety to the high-end students. The low group would get an abbreviated version of geometry and a second and third dose of multiplication for these three weeks prior to winter break.

The goal is to provide the low group with sufficient drill in multiplication that by the time students return to school in January, the whole class can begin Unit 5, "Dividing with Whole Numbers."

⑥ The writing assignments for this four-week block are a book report and a legend. The book report may be assigned from the universal ideas presented on page 42. The legend is tied to the science unit on earthquakes and volcanoes. Students will be creating a Native American legend explaining a natural phenomenon. Sample topics might include: earthquakes, volcanoes, waves, the tides, phases of the moon, rain, wind, or lightning.

⑦ As students continue reading their novel and complete the science unit on geology, an important social studies unit is in midstream — American Independence and the Revolution. This is the basis for two writing assignments, describing a historical location and fighting for a cause.

The first essay would be classified as descriptive. Students should be well versed in how to write descriptively since they have finished their study of adjectives, verbs, and are currently studying adverbs.

The second essay places students in a situation similar to early American patriots who believed in and fought for a cause. Students must write about their commitment to a cause or belief.

⑧ Writing for this month includes another book report and an opportunity for students to apply what they have learned about report writing in language arts. The person each student selects to write about might be from the field of aeronautics or be an American patriot. There is also the link to the biography students recently completed.

This type of curriculum integration makes teacher planning much faster and more complete. It is almost impossible to accomplish this coordination between subject areas unless one does a year-long plan.

⑨ In math, the students have completed the units on division with one-place and two-place divisors. Students will probably have segregated themselves into two groups — those who have mastered division and those who are still having difficulty. The high-level group will complete the measurement unit while the low group will continue to practice division.

Some may be concerned that the students who are having trouble with math are not exposed to the geometry and measurement units. There is no reason why portions of these units are not presented to the group as a whole; however, it is fair to assume that a student who has not mastered multiplication or division is less inclined to be able to master all aspects of the geometry and measurement units.

The measurement unit gives the low group three more weeks to work on division. The goal is to bring the entire class together when they begin Unit 8, "Adding and Subtracting Fractions."

⑩ The focus of writing this month is on creating both a business and friendly letter. The instruction on how to write letters has been completed in language arts. Now students must apply what they have learned.

This is another example of a "two-fer." Students should improve on their second letter by using the teacher's suggestions from the first.

The letter home from the West links to the social studies unit on westward expansion. Students should imagine they are living or traveling westward in a wagon train or on horseback and write a letter home telling what life is like.

⑪ At this point in math, the class will again split into those who can compute fractions and those who need more practice. The chapter on ratio and percentage is taught to the high group, and the low group will get remediation in the four operations in fractions.

The end of the year will allow the teacher to bring the entire class together for a unit on statistics and probability.

This is a creative unit which allows for individual projects and games. This is a positive way to close the school year.

⑫   Writing for weeks thirty-one through thirty-four return to the universal book report concept that students used earlier in the year. The second assignment is not linked to the book report, but it provides an opportunity to have students to compare some aspects of the North and South. Sample assignments might be a comparison of food, dress, agriculture, ethics, military power, nationalism, lifestyles, music, or geography. There are sufficient topics that each student could write on a different subject.

⑬   The final writing assignments during the year link to the study of the rain forest. In these assignments, the student will have to imagine that he or she is lost and completely alone. The rain forest may be one possible setting. Other locations include the desert, at sea, on a deserted island, on a planet in space, in the north or south polar regions, in a swamp, or in a heavily forested area. The purpose is to have students try to imagine how they would survive within a specific ecosystem.

The second assignment is using the information from the first essay, but now students must deliver an oral report of what they would take with them if they hoped to survive in a given habitat.

The end of the school year is an outstanding time to assign an oral presentation. It requires no after-school grading by the teacher, papers are not turned in late since there are no papers to be handed to the teacher, and it fills classroom time with an educationally sound lesson while requiring almost no planning time. Oral presentations give the teacher

time to prepare for the close of school. It also links to the last unit of language arts instruction.

Other considerations in a year long plan include:

• Your school district probably has at least one week scheduled for administering standardized tests. Testing week needs to be scheduled into the year-long plan and during this week, some instruction will have to be omitted.

• Try to schedule your writing assignments to be collected at least one week (two weeks is better) prior to the closing of quarter grades. This will give you time to correct essays, collect and grade late assignments, and this planned span of time will take pressure off of you.

• We all have personal as well as professional obligations. If you know that you have family commitments or personal necessities which will require your missing school, the year-long plan can be structured around these obligations. Again, this long-range planning is a great stress reliever.

Step 4: Creating Universal Assignments

The final step in the year long plan is creating lessons which can be used multiple times. This concept is described in the chapter on Universal Homework. A sample month-long universal assignment sheet is presented in the chapter entitled: Year-long Planning, Part Two.

Universal Homework

Homework has become as much of a part of the educational program as reading or math instruction. For the students, it provides a means to extend the school day and to practice the lessons presented in class.

For teachers, however, homework has become 25 percent education and 75 percent bookkeeping. Creating the homework assignment, assuring that students know the process before they leave, correcting and collecting the homework the next day, tracking down late papers, disciplining those who do not do their work, and contacting parents of non-performing students are the realities of homework in today's classroom. **Unfortunately, only a few of these activities have anything to do with teaching.**

Parents expect that their children will have homework; students expect to do homework. There are not enough hours in the teaching day to present lessons and provide students with sufficient practice time to master skills; therefore, we will continue to assign homework.

I believe we need to alter the type of homework we assign. If we make this one fundamental change, planning time will be dramatically reduced. Homework assignments should be:

1. Non-dependent upon that day's instruction.

2. Multi-night assignments which do not require daily bookkeeping.
3. Repetitive in nature from one month/week to the next.

If you use this approach, you will find you will spend more of your in-class time teaching and eliminate at least 50 percent of the pointless bookkeeping you are doing.

How does it work?

Let us begin with universal homework in spelling. Typically, on any given night during the week, your students will write spelling words a specific number of times, write the words in sentences, maybe create a word search or do some other activity you have created. If you are using a spelling book, you may assign spelling pages, and some teachers may create a spelling homework sheet with scrambled spelling words and other activities.

Two sets of universal spelling plan ideas are shown on the next several pages. There are seven choices for second graders and nine choices for seventh graders. Undoubtedly, you have other ideas which could be added.

In keeping with a concept discussed earlier, I believe we should decide how often we will begin a new spelling unit and then double that time frame. Most teachers in elementary schools teach spelling units for one week. I suggest you combine two one-week units and begin teaching spelling in two-week blocks of time. This gives students the opportunity to do different activities and eliminates some of the tedious routine of doing the same spelling activity every Monday night. It also allows the teacher to develop a two-week spelling plan which will be repeated eighteen times during the year rather

Spelling Activites Page *(for second grade)*

Using the words on this week's spelling list, complete one spelling activity each night. I will check your homework each day to be certain it is complete, but I will not collect the three activities until Thursday. *(My notes or side comments to the teacher are written in italics.)*

Idea 1:   Fold your paper three times (as shown in class) and write each spelling word three times with your right hand and then three more times with your left hand.

Idea 2:   Using different color pens or markers, write each spelling word as a complete word, but write each syllable in the word in a different color. For example, the word careless might have **care** written in red and **less** written in blue.

Idea 3:   Write each spelling word in a sentence. Each sentence must be at least 7 words in length. *(Additional requirements might be added to this activity from one month to the next. For example: Each sentence must at least 10 words. Each sentence must be a question.)*

Idea 4:   Fold your paper into three columns. In the center column write all of the spelling words. In the left hand column, write a word that rhymes with the spelling word. In the right hand column, write the word that means the same thing as the spelling word (synonym). *(Middle grade teachers might have students print in one column and use cursive in the next.)*

Idea 5:   Write a paragraph which contains eight spelling words. Imagine that your paragraph will be used as a test so you should misspell five of the words on purpose for classmates to find and correct. Be clever. Don't make the mistakes too easy to find.

Idea 6:   Draw letter boxes for each word on your spelling list. For example, **today** would look like:

Idea 7:   Make a tape recording on which you say the spelling word, pause for three seconds, and then spell the word correctly. We will play some of these tapes in class for practice.

Spelling Activites Page *(for Seventh Grade)*

Using the words on this week's spelling list, complete one spelling activity each night. I will check your homework each day to be certain it is complete, but I will not collect the three activities until Thursday. *(My notes or side comments to the teacher are written in italics.)*

Idea 1:   Fold your paper four times (as shown in class), and write each spelling word three times with your right hand and then three more times with your left hand.

Idea 2:   Using your spelling words as the lines in a drawing, "draw" a scene on a blank sheet of paper. Write each spelling word five times as you complete your picture.

Idea 3:   Using different color pens or markers, write each spelling word as a complete word, but write each syllable in the word in a different color. For example, the word "mythical" might have **myth** written in red, **i** written in blue, and **cal** written in orange.

Idea 4:   Write each spelling word in a sentence. Each sentence must be at least 10 words in length. *(Additional requirements might be added to this activity from one month to the next. For example: Each sentence must have a prepositional phrase. Each sentence must be compound. Each sentence must be written in past tense.)*

Idea 5:   Fold your paper in half and then fold it in half again. You will now have four columns. Write **noun** at the top of the first column, **verb** on the second, **adjective** on the third, and **adverb** on the fourth. Write each of your spelling words in the correct column and then change the word to a different part of speech and write it in the proper column. For example: The spelling word **different** would be written in the adjective column; then write **differently** in the adverb column or **difference** in the noun column.

Idea 6:   Fold your paper in half vertically (hot dog) and write all the spelling words in the column on the left. In the right-hand column, write the part of speech (noun, verb, etc.) of each spelling word.

32

Idea 7:   Write a paragraph which contains all spelling words. Imagine that your paragraph will be used as a test so you should deliberately misspell ten of the words for classmates to identify and correct. Be clever. Don't make the errors obvious.

Idea 8:   Fold your paper into three columns. In the center column write all of the spelling words. In the left hand column, add prefixes to the spelling words, in the right hand column add suffixes to the words.

Idea 9:   Create a mnemonic or trick to help remember how to spell ten of the words on your list. For example, in "mathematics," students often forget the "e." Remember, *"Ma, the ma ticks" have little ticks*. Often, the cornier or more extreme, the easier it is to remember.

than a one week plan which is repeated thirty-six times per year. Planning for one week or two weeks takes almost the same amount of time. Here is an example of a two week spelling homework plan:

Monday	Tuesday	Wednesday	Thursday	Friday
Do activities one or two	Do activity five	Do one spelling activity	Do one spelling activity	No Spelling homework
Monday	Tuesday	Wednesday	Thursday	Friday
Do one spelling activity	No Spelling homework	Spelling words with vocabulary	Spelling Pre-test	Spelling Test in school

In this case, students are given a choice of which activities to complete. Your homework assigment sheet will look exactly the same in May as in September. Do not assign specific pages, and do not create a spelling worksheet page each week. Instead, give students a choice of which activity they will complete on any given night.

It is also not essential to give homework every night in every subject. By building non-homework nights into the schedule, you gain freedom to allow students to complete the required spelling work should assemblies, field trips, or absences cut into your instructional time.

When students arrive in class the day after finishing one activity, do a quick check as to whether or not the homework is complete, and wait until Tuesday or Wednesday of the second week to collect a packet of student spelling work. Students should staple the homework pages together.

If you are having students complete pages in a spelling book, make this an in-class activity and use the work book pages for directed instruction. This eliminates the need to collect and correct these exercises. The other benefit is that I find the directions in spelling books are notoriously difficult to understand. When you use these as in-class lessons, you can explain, alter, or expand upon the directions.

Some other possible ideas to incorporate into this plan:

- If there are specific activities you want students to do, add, "You must do activity three," to your homework assignment sheet.

- If some activities seem easier than others, assign each activity a point value, and tell students they must do thirty or fifty points worth of assignments.

- If you are concerned about students copying work from one another, have them place their completed homework in their mailbox or in a classroom folder each day. After all assignments have been completed, have them staple them together and hand them to you.

- Use the student misspelling paragraph as part of your test. State testing no longer tests "spelling" the way we teach it. It is a proofreading test. Let your students create the test for you.

What does this plan accomplish?

The benefits of this approach are numerous:

1. Planning time for homework is almost non-existent. All of your time can be spent on preparing for in-class teaching.

2. Students have a choice. The creative students can do something more interesting than simply writing words numerous times.

3. You do not have to worry about students who have not completed work each day. Remind them that they must make up any missed work by collection day. If they do not complete their work, that is when you contact parents.

4. Daily bookkeeping — collecting, checking in, grading, and returning is eliminated for two, three, or four days per week.

5. When you do collect a packet, check quickly for completetion and grade one of the three activites (only giving minor points to the other papers). You do not need to grade them all. If a student's work is incomplete or sloppy, subtract points from the overall packet grade.

6. Absentees and independent study students can complete all homework even though they are not in class (the fundamental objective of universal homework).

Universal homework in various teaching settings

The spelling homework sheet is one sample and rather than go into depth with other applications, here is an overview of how universal homework can be assigned in a variety of teaching settings.

Vocabulary development

Almost all teachers teach vocabulary in one form or another. It may be terms related to science or social studies, SAT or ACT vocabulary preparation, new terms related to geometry or measurement in mathematics, literary terms, general knowledge, or a variety of other applications. In any of these situations, the universal homework sheet remains similar to that in spelling. Provide choices for students, assign activities over several nights and collect a packet of student work at the end.

A sample vocabulary activity list is shown on the next page. This same set of activites can be used in any setting. For second graders, the activities would be simplified, and for high school seniors, more sophistication would be added, however, for the many years I have used this approach, I find students very willing to complete at least three of these ideas.

The added benefit of this approach is that when students complete their work, reading their poems aloud, playing the tapes in class, using their tests as the class test for a unit exam, or allowing them to present the David Letterman list provides reinforcement for the vocabulary you are trying to teach. The more they hear it in different forms, the better they will remember it.

Vocabulary Activities

You may choose any three of the listed activities. Please choose activities that you think will help you remember the meanings of the words.

Idea 1: This is very basic. You may simply write a sentence using each word, name, and phrase. Each sentence must demonstrate that you know the correct meaning of the word.

Idea 2: Write a poem using at least twelve of the words. Your poem must rhyme in some type of pattern AND must be at least twelve lines long.

Idea 3: Make an audio tape recording of a play or a some type of presentation of the vocabulary words. You need to use all of the words and the tape WILL be played aloud in class for all to hear. I encourage you to give this one a try — I have a few microphones that you may borrow.

Idea 4: Make up a crossword puzzle using at least sixteen of the words. If you have one of the crossword puzzle programs for your computer this one is pretty easy. I may even use your puzzle as the test!

Idea 5: Make up a test using all of the words. Creativity counts here. Don't just write the word and leave a blank for fill in. Do matching, multiple choice, fill in the blank, etc.

Idea 6: Write a creative story using twenty of the words. Please underline them. This is a fairly easy task considering all of the words are on a similar topic.

Idea 7: Write a letter to one of the people on the vocabulary list. You must use proper letter format, and it must be at least three complete paragraphs. Use at least sixteen of the words. I would especially like to see some humor in this assignment.

Idea 8: Write each word in a column. In a second column, write a synonym for each word and in a third column, write an antonym for each word. You may leave six blank spaces.

Idea 9: Create an outline and categorize these words into common groups. You should create the heading (I, II, III, topics) and the vocabulary words will the A, B, C, subtopics. I will explain this more in class.

Idea 10: Write 20 of the vocabulary words In a list and opposite each word, write the name of a person who exemplifies that word. For example: refinement: Henry Ford.

Idea 11: Make a set of flashcards with the vocabulary words on one side and the definition or a synonym on the other. Neatness is essential.

Idea 12: Make up a top ten list (a la David Letterman) using at least one vocabulary word in each item.

Idea 13: Draw pictures which symbolize the meaning of fifteen of the words. For extra credit, make the picture a unified scene.

Book Reports

Most self-contained classroom teachers have their students write book reports. There are a variety of ways in which students can write them; however, I suggest teachers try to combine book reports into their science and social studies programs. By having students read books relevant to the area of study in content areas, several nights of homework each month can focus on reading and writing — paragraph by paragraph — the book report for that month.

Consider alternating each month (or three weeks) between a science-based book, a social studies-based book, and a book focusing on literature.

Most teachers would agree that one of the most valuable homework assignments is to have students read or have parents read to their children. A second, very positive homework assignment is having students write, given a specific assignment. Using book reports in the content subject areas is a realistic application.

For younger children, a combination of the approaches suggested on the next page would work well. If I were teaching second through fourth grade, I would have students write a book report of three paragraphs in length — each paragraph on a different aspect. For example, first paragraph, "What was the best thing about this book?" Second paragraph, "What character/setting/event was the most memorable? Which created the most vivid picture in your mind?" Third paragaph, "Is there a different ending you could create or is there something the author left out that you would like to know?"

This becomes a three-night project in which student samples can be read and discussed in class each day, and the

final product need not be collected until the three paragraphs are written (in neatest printing or cursive). The teacher can extend the process into a second week of homework by doing editing practice and possibly keyboarding skills during computer lab time.

For older students, the book report is a major writing assignment with very specific instructions about its structure. Remember, the goal is to enable students to do this at home without your having explained the homework in class that day. Once again, the assignment is given over one or two weeks' time. Students should bring paragraphs to class each day which can be read aloud and discussed.

You can allow students to choose which idea they will use, or you may assign a specific idea for the entire class.

Science Chapter Assignments

In developing this section, I reviewed science books from third, eighth, tenth and twelfth grades. The striking element was the similarity in the ways in which these books were structured. Typically there are six to eight units with three or four chapters per unit. Each chapter has a set of questions which check for understanding and a second set which asks students to apply their knowledge to other situations. Units also typically present a set of vocabulary words.

A teacher who does not readily identify with topics in science would have a tremendous amount of work to do to prepare experiments, lessons, and demonstrations in addition to collecting materials for the classroom. Without some simplified approach to providing homework, one could spend far too much time in preparation.

Book Report Ideas

This year you will write a book report every other month on a book you have chosen from the library. Since the type of book you select from month to month may vary, you have a choice of the type of book report you will write. In addition to the actual report, you must also complete one of the "brainstorm" activities.

Idea 1: Write a four to five paragraph essay in which you explain the plot, the characters, and what you learned from reading this book. In the closing paragraph, make a recommendation as to whether a person should or should not take the time to read the book. Explain why (or why not).

Idea 2: Write a letter to one of the characters in the book. In this letter, begin by introducing yourself, then write a paragraph explaining how you are similar or different than the character. In the third paragraph, tell how you would have handled a situation differently (give advice or admit your poor judgement or inexperience). In the closing paragraph, tell the character what you think of him or her.

Idea 3: Create a new or different ending for the book. Begin by describing what actually happens in the end. In the next paragraph explain the different ending, and in the closing paragraph, tell why your ending would or would not be more successful.

Idea 4: Imagine that you are a close friend of one of the characters in the book. Begin with a paragraph which describes how you met. In the next two paragraphs describe what females and males think of this character, and in the closing, tell what it is like to have this person as a close friend.

Idea 5: Write a book review which might appear in a newpaper or magazine. Review the book explaining what, where, who, when, why, and how.

BRAINSTORM IDEAS:

1. Design a new cover jacket for the book.

2. Draw a scene from the book.

3. Create an advertisement which might appear in a magazine which tries to convince people to buy and read the book.

Science universal homework assignments are presented in two different forms. On this page, assignments are in a list format as might be written on the board or on a weekly assignment sheet. They are generic assignments which need only page numbers inserted in the blanks.

On the following pages, a six-week calendar shows how I would prepare homework assignment for a complete science unit.

The calendar on page 44 (October 25 through 28) reference the "Essential Understanding" or "EU." This concept is explained on pages 50 through 54.

- Reread pages ___ through ___ and answer questions _____ in complete sentences.

- Write ten facts which you learned as you read pages ___ through ___.

- After reading pages ___ through ___ create a ten question matching test using important names or vocabulary.

- Reread pages ___ through ___ , and using the bold face section titles as Roman numeral headings, list at least three important ideas from that section.

- Using the vocabulary list in the chapter review section, create eight multiple choice questions.

- After reading pages ___ through ___ , write one paragraph of no more than seventy-five words which would explain the important concepts to an eight year old.

- Write a paragraph or two identifying an occupation which would require expertise in the field of science we are studying. Explain

(Continued on page 46)

Science

September 20 - October 29

Monday	Tuesday	Wednesday	Thursday	Friday
Sep 20 HW: Review pages 6-9 and complete one activity.	**Sep 21** HW: Review pages 10-12 and complete one activity.	**Sep 22** HW: Review pages 13-16 and complete one activity.	**Sep 23** HW: Answer Sum it Up questions 1 & 4.	**Sep 24** HW: Copy chapter 1 vocabulary in your spiral notebook and write a short definition for each word.
Sep 27 HW: Review pages 19-21 and complete one activity.	**Sep 28** HW: Review pages 22-24 and complete one activity.	**Sep 29** HW: Review pages 26-29 and complete one activity.	**Sep 30** HW: Write a 50 word response to Challenge Question 3 on page 31.	**Oct 1** HW: Copy chapter 2 vocabulary in your spiral notebook and write a short definition for each word.
Oct 4 HW: Review pages 32-34 and complete one activity.	**Oct 5** HW: Review pages 35-37 and complete one activity.	**Oct 6** HW: Review pages 38-41 and complete one activity.	**Oct 7** HW: Review pages 41-44 and complete one activity.	**Oct 8** HW: Copy chapter 3 vocabulary in your spiral notebook and write a short definition for each word.
Oct 11 HW: Write a description of the process used in one of the experiments of the past three weeks.	**Oct 12** HW: Over the next two nights, describe an occupation that would need to know the science we are studying. Explain why.	**Oct 13**	**Oct 14** HW: Over the next two nights, describe the work of a famous scientist in the field we are studying.	**Oct 15**
Oct 18 HW: Complete one vocabulary activity.	**Oct 19** HW: Complete one vocabulary activity.	**Oct 20** HW: Complete one vocabulary activity.	**Oct 21** HW: Write a 100 to 125 word paragraph explaining why/how the science we are studying affects your life.	**Oct 22**
Oct 25 HW: Write a 75 to 100 word paragraph explaining your essential understanding (EU) question.	**Oct 26** HW: Write a 75 to 100 word paragraph on any one of the four remaining EU questions.	**Oct 27** HW: Using the EU questions responses given in class, add at least two unit vocabulary words to each response.	**Oct 28** HW: Study the EU questions and vocabulary for tomorrow's test.	**Oct 29** **METEOROLOGY UNIT TEST**

Science Meteorology Unit

Duplicate on the back of the homework calendar

Review Activity Choices: You may not repeat any activity within one week.

1. Outline the assigned pages using the bold headings as Roman numerals.

2. Create a chapter test with a ten question matching section and four multiple choice items.

3. Write a list of ten reasons why it is important to learn the information in this chapter.

4. Using this chapter's new vocabulary words as search prompts, find three websites which provide more information. Write two facts you learned from visiting each website.

5. In 75 words or more, describe an invention which would allow scientists to instantly learn more about the subject in the assigned pages.

6. Choose the most important concept in the assigned pages and write an explanation in seventy-five words or less which would explain the concept to a young child.

7. Choose a concept from the assigned pages and then describe how this applies to a "real life" situation. Make a comparison.

Vocabulary Activity Choices:

1. Make a set of flashcards with at least eight words from the assigned pages. Write the word on one side and a definition and picture demonstrating the meaning of the word on the reverse.

2. Using the unit vocabulary, create a crossword puzzle.

3. Write a word chain which connects at least twelve of the words. For example, a hemisphere is similar to the equator in that the equator divides Earth into two hemispheres. The equator is like... et cetera. Each word should connect or have a relationship to the previous word.

4. Draw pictures which demonstrate the meaning of the words. The word itself must appear in the picture.

45

why the information you learned would be necessary in this occupation.

- Write a list of ten words which might be used to find information about this field of science on the internet and then write a ranking (1-10) of which words would provide the most valuable information.

- Brainstorm a list of ten reasons why it is important to study and know about this particular field of science. Write your reasons in complete sentences.

- Create an invention that would enable scientists in this field of study to instantly learn more about this topic. Describe the invention, and explain why it hasn't already been developed.

Social Studies Chapter Assignments

Just as science books share similarities between grade levels, so do social studies texts. The books I reviewed typically had eight to ten units and were divided into three to five chapters per unit. It would seem to be a real challenge to complete an entire social studies text in a year. Each grade level book presents more material and more reading than hours in the teaching day permit. This concern has been discussed previously in the chapter on year-long planning.

Many of the universal activities that will work for science function equally well for social studies. Since history adds the elements of geography, historical names, and chronology, there are many new possibilities.

Included below, for convenience sake, are some repeat ideas from science. Then additional questions are presented and another sample homework assignment sheet is included.

- Reread pages ___ through ___ and answer questions _____ in complete sentences.

- Write ten facts which you learned as you read pages ____ through ____.

- After reading pages ____ through ____ create a ten question matching test using important names, places, or vocabulary.

- Reread pages ____ through ____. Using the bold face section titles as Roman numeral headings, list at least three important ideas from that section.

- Using the vocabulary list in the chapter review section, create eight multiple choice questions.

- After reading pages ____ through ____, write one paragraph of no more than seventy-five words which would explain the importance of one of the chapter's people or places. Write this in words that would make sense to an eight year old.

- Write a letter of at least one hundred words imagining that you are one of the historical figures in this chapter. This letter should be addressed to your spouse or children. Explain why what you are doing is important to you and to them.

- Write a list of ten words which might be used to find information about this historical period on the internet and then write a ranking (1-10) of which words would provide the most valuable information.

- Choosing one of the important events in this chapter, write the names of two people in other periods of history who perhaps were confronted with a similar situation. Explain how the circumstances were the same.

(Continued on page 50)

47

Social Studies

September 20 - October 22

Monday	Tuesday	Wednesday	Thursday	Friday
Sep 20 HW: Review pages 7-14 and complete one activity.	**Sep 21** Homework: Map Letter Internet Cartoon Song/Rhyme	**Sep 22** HW: Review pages 16-24 and complete one activity.	**Sep 23** HW: Review pages 25-33 and complete one activity.	**Sep 24** Homework: Map Letter Internet Cartoon Song/Rhyme
Sep 27 HW: Review pages 37-45 and complete one activity.	**Sep 28** Homework: Map Letter Internet Cartoon Song/Rhyme	**Sep 29** HW: Review pages 46-55 and complete one activity.	**Sep 30** Homework: Map Letter Internet Cartoon Song/Rhyme	**Oct 1** HW: Review pages 56-64 and complete one activity.
Oct 4 Homework: Map Letter Internet Cartoon Song/Rhyme	**Oct 5** HW: Review pages 65-76 and complete one activity.	**Oct 6** Homework: Map Letter Internet Cartoon Song/Rhyme	**Oct 7** HW: Review pages 79-88 and complete one activity.	**Oct 8** HW: Complete one vocabulary activity.
Oct 11 HW: Complete one vocabulary activity.	**Oct 12** HW: Complete one vocabulary activity.	**Oct 13** Homework: Person, Place, Event Report	**Oct 14**	**Oct 15**
Oct 18 HW: Write a 75 to 100 word paragraph explaining your essential understanding (EU) question.	**Oct 19** HW: Write a 75 to 100 word paragraph on any one of the four remaining EU questions.	**Oct 20** HW: Using the EU questions responses given in class, add at least two unit vocabulary words to each response.	**Oct 21** HW: Study the EU questions and vocabulary for tomorrow's test.	**Oct 22** UNIT TEST THE FALL OF ROME

World History Unit - The Fall of Rome

Duplicate on the back of the calendar

Review Activity Choices: You may not repeat any activity within one week.

1. Outline the assigned pages using the bold headings as Roman numerals.
2. Create a chapter test with a ten question matching section and four multiple choice items.
3. Write a list of ten reasons why it is important to learn the information in this chapter.
4. Using this chapter's new vocabulary words as search prompts, find three websites which provide more information. Write two facts you learned from visiting each website.
5. In seventy-five words or more, describe an invention which exists today which would have resolved a problem or conflict presented in the assigned pages.
6. Choose the most important concept in the assigned pages, and write an explanation in seventy-five words or less which would explain the concept to a young child.
7. Choose a concept from the assigned pages, and describe how this parallels a situation in the world today.

Vocabulary Activity Choices:

1. Make a set of flashcards with at least eight words from the assigned pages. Write the word on one side and a definition and picture demonstrating the meaning of the word on the reverse.
2. Using the unit vocabulary, create a crossword puzzle.
3. Write a word chain which connects at least twelve of the words. For example, a hemisphere is similar to the equator in that the equator divides Earth into two hemispheres. The equator is like... et cetera.
4. Draw pictures which demonstrate the meaning of the words. The word itself must appear in the picture.

- To the tune of a children's song, write one verse which might have been a folksong of the time. You may also write a nursery rhyme such as, "Hey diddle, diddle..." Your song or rhyme should reflect the mood of the people during this period of history.

- Draw a political cartoon which represents one of the conflicts or situations described in this chapter.

- Create a map of your own which demonstrates some aspect of the concepts taught in this chapter.

- Create a list of ten questions you would ask one of the historical figures in this chapter if you were a television newsperson.

- Write a brief speech (about one hundred words) that one of the historical figures in this chapter might deliver. Try to make it inspirational, almost as though it is a coach's motivational message.

- Do some research to try to find a fad, game, toy, song, book, hobby, dance, unusual food or beverage, fashion, slogan, collectable, or currency which was in vogue during this time in history.

Science and Social Studies Test Week

Within any science or social studies unit, there are between three and seven "essential understandings." These concepts, along with vocabulary, geography, and names, are typically the focus of the test for that section. As test week approaches in these content areas, the same universal homework schedule can be used.

To have every student write numerous paragraphs on a test is unnecessary. Each student need only write on one of

the essential understandings. This makes correcting much faster and forces us into focusing upon the important content during classtime. The homework and classwork schedule for the week is as follows:

Monday

In class: 1. Review vocabulary, names, and places.

2. Have students copy the three to seven key questions which are written on the board. Let them know that these are the questions they will need to answer on Friday's test.

3. Count students off to write on a specific questions. For example, if there are five "essential understanding" questions, count students off, "1, 2, 3, 4, 5, 1, 2, 3,... etc." All of the "one's" write on question one, the "two's" on question two, etc.

Homework: 1. Write a paragraph explaining a key question.

Tuesday

In class: 1. All "one's" meet in a group (or two if there are too many). All "two's" meet in another group The object is to have each group member read his or her paragraph and then have one group member write a "perfect" answer using the best components of each group member's homework.

2. Upon completion, one member of each group should read the paragraph aloud. Briefly discuss each paragraph after it is read to add or delete information.

3. Collect all group generated questions.

Homework 1. Students complete a vocabulary activity or do one of the tests that was created earlier in the study of the unit.

Wednesday

In class:

1. Cut, paste, and duplicate Tuesday's group responses. All five question responses should be given to each student.

2. Distribute duplicated group responses to read aloud. Have students read paragraphs aloud and identify what is good and what needs embellishment.

3. Correct Tuesday night's sample test.

Homework:

1. Have students select another question or count off students to write on a second question. Remind them that this is for Friday's test.

2. Offer bonus points to any student who will bring Wednesday night's homework to you before school begins on Thursday.

Thursday

In class:

1. Before class, cut, paste, and duplicate the very best responses from Wednesday's homework. Duplicate on a different color paper.

2. Review vocabulary, locations, and names. Have students add these to the duplicated question responses.

Homework:

1. Study the model paragraphs for Friday's test.

Friday

In class:

1. Administer test, but each student need only write on one of the key questions. Other test items might include objective questions on vocabulary, geography, dates, or names.

This approach accomplishes a number of objectives. First, the most important components of any content area unit are the essential understandings. There is no point in teaching a

science unit if students walk away with only factual information. They must be able to explain what they have learned. Reiterating these explanations by writing them, listening to, and reading quality examples cannot help but to increase learning. Low-end students learn more, and high-end students embellish and synthesize.

Second, this approach gives every student an opportunity to be successful. If on Monday, the teacher were to write five essay questions on the board and give no further support, many students in the room would give up. It is too much to remember. Some students may still choose to "tune out," but at least you have given them an equal opportunity. In my experience in using this approach, every student, even those who still do poorly on the test, know more than they would have without using this procedure. It is an equalizer.

Third, if you do not assign science or social studies homework every night, the approach will still work if students complete only Monday night's homework. Once we have student samples, we can do the discussion and embellishment in class.

Fourth, teacher planning during test week is minimal and focused instruction is at a maximum level. You are teaching and practicing precisely what students need to know.

The concerns I hear when I first present this approach at workshops are:

Don't students just memorize the answers and feed it back to you?

Some do, but many, especially the high end students, add ideas to make their responses unique. I encourage them to do this. For the students who struggle, there is a degree of rote

memorization; however, I do not see a problem with this because they are motiviated by their success and grade. Without this help, their scores would be very low.

Don't all the students get A's?

I wish this were true, but no matter how much help we give students, they always seem to distribute themselves into A's, B's, C's, and lower. What I do find is that there are far fewer failing grades. The A students get higher A's and the F students get C's and D's. It just seems to work out this way.

Doesn't it get monotonous to use the same approach over and over?

I would only use this for the **unit** examinations in social studies and science. If there are six units in each content area, this testing week approach will only be used twelve times during the year. There are many activities which are repeated more often than this.

Writing a Report about a Person, Place, Thing or Location

Students typically do "reports" of various kinds. In elementary school these reports may be on topics such as presidents, states, countries, cities, celebrities, monuments, buildings, mammals, flowers, dinosaurs, birds, inventions, and national parks. If it is a noun, kids write reports about it.

Rather than creating a different format every time students do a report, this can become a generic homework/

classwork assignment in which students choose different components appropriate to the topic. The same explanation can be used for any report regardless of subject.

Report Writing

Over the next week, you will be writing a report on _____ . This sheet describes twelve possible ingredients you may include in your report. You must use ideas 1 and 12. In addition, please choose four of the remaining ideas in your finished paper. As you will see, not all ideas will apply to every topic.

1. What is your topic and why is it important or interesting?

2. When and where was this topic first discovered or begun?

3. How has this influenced your life or changed the way in which you live?

4. Tell three of the most interesting things you learned about this topic.

5. What are some other topics which are in the same family, species, or are in some way similar to the topic. How are they alike and in what ways are they different?

6. Choose a character you have seen in a movie or on television who reminds you of the topic you are describing. Tell at least two ways in which they are the same.

7. Describe why your topic is now old fashioned or no longer modern. What happened to change people's knowledge or opinion?

8. What is the worst or most negative thing you learned about your topic?

9. Do a survey in which you create five questions about your topic. Ask five people these questions, and write a paragraph explaining the results of your survey.

10. Draw a map which shows the location you are describing.

11. Do a drawing, portrait, or artistic representation of your topic.

12. In your closing paragraph, write one or two sentences that are like an advertisement for your topic. Convince the reader why he or she should try to learn more about your topic.

In addition to these twelve basic ideas, the teacher may wish to add two or three specific ideas for each report. Also included should be guidelines concerning length of paragraphs, overall length of the finished assignment, and style of presentation. A requirement I have used to eliminate the possiblity of students copying a report from the internet or from an encyclopedia is to insist that it be written in first person. The use of "I" forces students to reword researched information.

Foreign Language

As a Spanish teacher, I felt compelled to include this section. There may not be a lot of us, but we face the same dilemma with homework as most teachers do. We typically have worksheets and book exercises that can be used as homework; however, I prefer to provide universal homework that a student can complete even if he or she were not in class that day.

I try to cover a textbook chapter every two weeks. This allows me to to complete all fifteen required chapters by the close of third quarter. The fourth quarter is a review of each chapter, beginning again with Chapter 1. This "double dose" has been a very successful method.

By completing a chapter every two weeks, I apply my technique of doubling and actually plan for a month at a time. As one can see from the monthly calendar on the next page, the two-week block repeats itself. Included on the monthly assignment sheets are lists of the new vocabulary and the fifteen sentences to be translated.

The two-day homework assignment which students complete on Monday and Tuesday of the second week is an application of that chapter's content. For example, Chapter 1 uses a number of words dealing with food, so the two-day assignments is to create a restaurant menu. Chapter 2 words feature descriptive adjectives. The two-day project is to find four pictures in magazines — a man, a woman, a dog, and a cat (bird or fish). The students must then write two to three sentences describing each of these pictures.

The benefit of this approach is as in all universal homework, the student need not be in class to complete the assignment.

I have used this approach in one form or another for many years. My students do not find it tedious or repetitious. If they choose to complete all homework in one night, I see that as being resourceful. The most positive outcome is that very few students come to class unprepared. I have eliminated most of their excuses. I save time in both planning and record keeping.

Spanish

Monday	Tuesday	Wednesday	Thursday	Friday
Sep 20 Homework Practice vocabulary with your method	**Sep 21** Homework Write eight sentences with three different new vocabulary words per sentence	**Sep 22** Homework Translate Five Sentences	**Sep 23** Homework Translate Five Sentences	**Sep 24** Homework Translate Five Sentences
Sep 27 Homework - You have two days to complete the project described last week in class. Extra points will be rewarded for going above and beyond the basic requirements	**Sep 28**	**Sep 29** Homework Practice Dialogue for tomorrow	**Sep 30** Homework Complete vocabulary study sheet and study for test	**Oct 1** CHAPTER TEST
Oct 4 Homework Practice vocabulary with your method	**Oct 5** Homework Write eight sentences with three different new vocabulary words per sentence	**Oct 6** Homework Translate Five Sentences	**Oct 7** Homework Translate Five Sentences	**Oct 8** Homework Translate Five Sentences
Oct 11 Homework - You have two days to complete the project described last week in class. Extra points will be rewarded for going above and beyond the basic requirements	**Oct 12**	**Oct 13** Homework Practice Dialogue for tomorrow	**Oct 14** Homework Complete vocabulary study sheet and study for test	**Oct 15** CHAPTER TEST

Chapter 1 Sentences

1. Which do you like more, tacos, or hamburgers?
2. You like to cook, right?
3. What do you like to do, play baseball or play guitar?
4. There are many students in class.
5. With whom do you like to study?
6. How many chairs and tables are there in class?
7. I love to help at home and at school.
8. I don't like sports but I love to dance.
9. Which do you like to eat, french fries or cheese sandwiches?
10. I don't like soccer but I love American football.
11. There are six sodas and four salads on the table.
12. Do you like ham sandwiches with or without butter?
13. Is there popular or classical music here?
14. Then why don't you like to listen to the radio?
15. Oh yes, I like to practice the piano.

Chapter 2 Sentences

1. Are there many students in your Spanish class?
2. I am red headed, and you are brunette.
3. What do you like more, salad or hamburgers.
4. Do you like to read books in class on Fridays?
5. There isn't any ice cream at school today.
6. They are blonde, tall, and handsome and are from Canada.
7. The cats are very old, the dog is young, and the fish is enormous.
8. We are too tall and too fat to go to the United States.
9. She is also very good looking, right?
10. Do you like to help at home, or do you like to play sports?
11. The young man is handsome, and the young women are pretty.
12. My dog is very small, but my cat is enormous.
13. My school friends are Spanish.
14. The man and woman are old, but they are rather handsome.
15. On the contrary, the bird is ugly and fat!

Chapter 1

la bandera	the flag
el cartel	the poster
el deporte	the sport
la ensalada	the salad
el escritorio	the desk
el examen	the test
el helado	the ice cream
el jamón	the ham
la leche	the milk
la limonada	the lemonade
la mantequilla	the butter
el mapa	the map
la mesa	the table
la música	the music
el pan	the bread
el periódico	the newspaper
el plato	the plate
el pupitre	the student desk
el queso	the cheese
el refresco	the soda
el sandwich	the sandwich
la silla	the chair
el taco	the taco
la tarea	the homework
la tiza	the chalk
muchos	many
pocos	few
popular	popular
ayudar	to help
estudiar	to study
lavar	to wash
practicar	to practice

entonces	then
más	more
mucho	much
con	with
para	for
sin	without
o	or
porque	because
pues	well then
¿con quién?	with whom
¿por qué?	why
¿quién?	who
¡ah, sí!	oh, yes
¡cómo no!	why not
en casa	at home
me encantan	I love (them)
me gustan	I like (them)
¿verdad?	really
el alumno	the student

Chapter 2

el amigo	the friend
la capital	the capital
el compañero	the schoolfriend
el gato	the cat
el hombre	the man
el muchacho	the boy
la mujer	the woman
el país	the country
el pájaro	the bird
el perro	the dog

el pez	the fish
los peces	the fish(es)
ellos(as)	they
nosotros	we
ustedes (Uds.)	"yous"
alto	tall
bajo	short
bonito	pretty
corto	short
delgado	skinny
enorme	enormous
español (a)	Spanish
feo	ugly
gordo	fat
grande	big
guapo	handsome
joven/jóvenes	young
largo	large
moreno	brunette
nuevo	new
pelirrojo	redhead
pequeño	small
rubio	blonde
viejo	old
ser	to be
bastante	rather/fairly/kind of
demasiado	too much
al contrario	on the contrary
¿cómo es ...?	how is
de origen	what origin
¿de qué país?	from what country

Literature

Book reports are typically written when students have finished reading the book, but many of us assign pages to be read as a homework assignment. Reading may be from a basal reader, a short story collection, or from a novel. How can we be certain that students are actually doing the reading?

If reading assignments are a part of a homework plan, I recommend a blend of three universal homework approaches.

Once every other week, I would do oral questioning of students. There is no need to have every student take a written test. This takes too long to administer and even longer to correct. Instead, write down ten to fifteen questions ranging from recalling specific details to making inferences.

Randomly call on students to respond to these questions, giving a score of one to ten points for accuracy of answers. Every student will not have an opportunity to answer each session, but over the course of a month, each student will have at least one opportunity to demonstrate that he or she has read the required pages.

The benefit of oral testing is that other students hear responses and learn from them.

If oral questioning is done one day every other week, this can alternate with having students write a paragraph explaining or interpreting what they read the previous night. Let every student write, but only correct one of every four papers.

I refer to this process as the "paragraph lottery." It is a wonderful time saving technique. It is described in the chapter, "Twenty-five New Tips."

The third technique I suggest for universal homework assignments in literature is to give students the following list of activities. I would give them a choice of which activity they want to do on any given night. Because these ideas are so open-ended, it makes it very difficult for students to copy from one another.

Literature Homework Ideas

When you have finished reading the assigned pages, choose one of the following ideas to demonstrate that you understand what you have read.

Idea 1: Select two of the characters you read about, and write a short paragraph which compares their situation with the predicament faced by two people in a movie or television show. Explain how they are the same.

Idea 2: Draw an aerial view of the setting of the pages you read. Develop a legend for different characters or groups, and then draw lines with arrows to show how these characters moved about the scene.

Idea 3: Select the most important section of the pages read, and write a dialogue in today's vernacular which paraphrases the action.

Idea 4: Select ten vocabulary words which are highly descriptive or emotional, and then write a sentence for each word which explains why that word was appropriate to that situation.

Idea 5: Write a cryptic paragraph; that is, a choppy, non-descriptive set of sentences which explain the action in the pages you read. For example: "Thomas came home. He was mad, etc.."

Idea 6: Write a one or two stanza poem or a limerick which cleverly tells what occurred in the pages you read.

Idea 7: Create an outline as you read. Each Roman numeral should identify a different scene, dialogue, or conflict. These should be

placed in sequential order. Under each Roman numeral, list or briefly describe what happened.

Idea 8:   Write a paragraph which summarizes the pages you read. Be concise and include only the important details.

When checking to see if work is complete each day, I would ask students to hold up their papers to verify that work is finished. Ask for several volunteers or call on three or four students to share their work with the class. Many of these ideas produce interesting topics for discussion and many are also entertaining.

I would then have each student place his or her paper in an individual file folder, repeating this procedure each day. At the end of each week, have students staple their homework pages together and hand them in. Select one paper to correct from each student's packet.

Over a month-long study of a novel, a universal homework sheet might look like the calendar presented on the next page. Many of the pages listed for homework would be read in class, but any student who is absent would be able to complete the assignment.

In terms of grading this month-long project, one grade per week would be generated from the ideas completed at home, a second grade would come from the lottery paragraphs written in class (signified by "Quiz in Class Tomorrow") or the oral quiz (signified by "Quiz Tomorrow"), and there would be a test grade at the end.

Literature Homework Sheet
The Lion, the Witch, and the Wardrobe

Monday	Tuesday	Wednesday	Thursday	Friday
Sep 20 Finish Reading Chapter 1 Pgs. 1 - 8 Do one idea	**Sep 21** Read Chapter 2 Pgs. 9 - 19 Do one idea	**Sep 22** Read Chapter 3 Pgs. 20 - 28 Quiz Tomorrow	**Sep 23** Read Chapter 4 Pgs. 29 - 39 Do one idea	**Sep 24** Read Chapter 5 Pgs. 40 - 49 Do one idea
Sep 27 Read Chapter 6 Pgs. 50 - 59 Do one idea	**Sep 28** Read Chapter 7 Pgs. 60 - 71 Do one idea	**Sep 29** Read Chapter 8 Pgs. 72 - 83 Do one idea	**Sep 30** Read Chapter 9 Pgs. 84 - 94 Quiz in Class Tomorrow	**Oct 1** Read Chapter 10 Pgs. 95 - 106 Do one idea
Oct 4 Read Chapter 11 Pgs. 107 - 118 Do one idea	**Oct 5** Read Chapter 12 Pgs. 119 - 129 Quiz in Class Tomorrow	**Oct 6** Read Chapter 13 Pgs. 130 - 141 Do one idea	**Oct 7** Read Chapter 14 Pgs. 142 - 152 Quiz Tomorrow	**Oct 8** Read Chapter 15 Pgs. 153 - 163 Do one idea
Oct 11 Read Chapter 16 Pgs. 164 - 174 Do one idea	**Oct 12** Read Chapter 17 Pgs. 175 - 186 Do one idea	**Oct 13** Review test study sheet	**Oct 14** Test on Lion, Witch, & Wardrobe	**Oct 15**

Mathematics

The sequential progression of mathematics makes multi-week planning a challenge. One can list nightly assignments for a month-long period of time, but if students have not mastered a concept in class, the assigned homework for that night cannot be completed. This throws the entire schedule off for the remainder of the month.

There are two different approaches which one might adopt in applying universal homework in math. The first is rather traditional but avoids assigning actual calendar dates for each assignment; the second is radical in that it completely changes the way in which homework is assigned. I believe it is time to do something radically different in math.

When a teacher begins a new unit in mathematics, typically he or she will evaluate a chapter and develop a rough outline of how long each objective will take. If there are twelve units in a math book, it is safe to assume that each unit *should* take about four weeks.

As mentioned above, if we use a traditional calendar to list nightly assignments, we are often quickly off schedule due to students' learning pace. If you wish to coordinate in-class lessons with nightly homework, I suggest you use a spread-sheet. Each assignment is given a number, and should students fail demonstrate mastery in class, the homework might be altered or cancelled for that night. The next day would be spent reteaching the concept and the corresponding homework assignment number would be postponed accordingly.

Assign #	Topic	Homework	Date
1	Multiples of ten	Page 79, 1 - 5 and 10 - 21	
2	Estimating Products	Page 83, 1 - 22	
3	Problem Solving - Estimation	Page 85, 1 - 8	
4	Multiplying: one digit factors	Page 87, 11 - 30	
5	Multiplying larger number	Page 89, 1-23 odd	
6	Making change	Page 90, 1 - 7; Page 91, 1 - 4	
7	Multiplying: two digit factors	Page 93, 1 - 20	
8	Multiplying: two digit factors	Worksheet from class	
9	Multiplying: three digit factors	Page 95, 1 - 10	
10	Multiplying: three digit factors	Page 95, 11 - 24	
11	Problem Solving - two steps	Page 97, 1 - 9	
12	Chapter Review	Worksheet from class	
13	Practice Chapter Test	Worksheet from class	

While this method will work, it does not meet the criteria for "universal homework." In order for homework to be truly universal, the student need not be in class to know how to complete the assignment. The second approach does accomplish this goal. The fundamental precepts for this method are:

- All math homework is mixed-practice review.
- All students, regardless of grouping, do the same assignment.
- Students never practice what has been learned in class during that week.

If this sounds unrealistic, let's take a closer look before dismissing the concept.

First, when students apply what they have learned in math, it is rare to repeat a procedure or algorithm over and over. In real life (or standardized tests) we complete one type of problem and then move to another operation. We add, then multiply, then use a decimal or percent, etc. We must train our students to be flexible in applying math skills. They must see a problem, apply the process, find the answer, and encounter a different type of problem. Mixed practice provides this experience.

Second, we do not want a parent to teach a math process to the child at home. If our students have a homework assignment in math which is unclear to them; they will often ask their parents for help. My experience is that as well-meaning as parents may be, they often explain the process differently than I, they shortcut a step that is imperative for students to comprehend, or they teach the concept incorrectly. Worse yet, they complain that the teacher is not teaching it the right way. Regardless of the scenario, we, the teachers, lose!

I do not want my students doing a math procedure at home that they have not mastered in class.

Third, if all math homework is review, I can place my nightly homework assignments on a month-long calendar and never be thrown off schedule by the varied pace of student learning.

In addition, I can give the same homework to the entire class. There may be a set of four or eight problems that are beyond the ability of my low group. In this case, the homework says, "Group 1 do problems 1 - 16; group 2 do problems 1 - 10." When all students do the same work, we can correct more quickly and efficiently and record keeping is simplified.

The next dilemma is how to create all of this review practice. There are four methods that I recommend.

Create multiple homework sheets by omitting operation symbols. This process is very effective and is appropriate for all elementary and middle school grade levels. High school basic math teachers can use this as well.

On an 8½" by 11" sheet of paper, draw a set of lines as shown. I prefer to use only the front side of a sheet of paper since it is easier to correct and costs less to duplicate. Number squares 1 through 12, and create a space for the student's name (formatting this paper will save time when correcting this paper in the future).

The next couple of steps seem rather confusing, and for the sake of simplicity, I will provide only four sample problems rather than twelve. In each box write a set of numbers, arranged as they would be for a specific math operation (addition, subtraction, multiplication, or division). Do not write any operations symbols. Problems one through four might be:

①   ②   ③   ④

     125   4367 $\frac{1}{2}$ $\frac{1}{3}$ 89

       6   34

When you have filled in each of the twelve squares with a number set, duplicate twenty copies of the page. The next step is to write operation symbols, one page at a time. The trick is to vary each problem with a different symbol or an added number. Five sample variations are shown on the next page.

Variation 1

①
$$\begin{array}{r} 125 \\ -6 \\ \hline \end{array}$$

②
$$4\overline{)367}$$

③
$$\frac{1}{2} + \frac{1}{3} =$$

④
$$\begin{array}{r} 89 \\ \times 34 \\ \hline \end{array}$$

Variation 2

①
$$\begin{array}{r} 125 \\ \times6 \\ \hline \end{array}$$

②
$$43\overline{)67}$$

③
$$\frac{1}{2} \quad \frac{1}{3} =$$

④
$$\begin{array}{r} 89 \\ +34 \\ \hline \end{array}$$

Variation 3

①
$$\begin{array}{r} 125 \\ +56 \\ \hline \end{array}$$

②
$$4\overline{)36.7}$$

③
$$\frac{1}{2} \times \frac{1}{3} =$$

④
$$\begin{array}{r} 89 \\ -34 \\ \hline \end{array}$$

Variation 4

①
$$\begin{array}{r} 12.5 \\ +.6 \\ \hline \end{array}$$

②
$$5\overline{)4367}$$

③
$$1\frac{1}{2} + \frac{1}{3} =$$

④
$$\begin{array}{r} 89 \\ \times 3.4 \\ \hline \end{array}$$

Variation 5

①
$$\begin{array}{r} 125 \\ \times 356 \\ \hline \end{array}$$

②
$$4\overline{)3.67}$$

③
$$\frac{1}{2} - \frac{1}{3} =$$

④
$$\begin{array}{r} 68.9 \\ -3.4 \\ \hline \end{array}$$

Problems other than those shown can be created: measurement problems to compute area, perimeter, volume; percentage problems; telling time; graphs or grids with different values or scales; geometry formula problems; and a myraid of other possibilities.

In previous years, when teaching math, I used this technique to create worksheets. I could make twenty such sheets in about five minutes. By duplicating thirty copies of each and combining them with the techniques to follow, I typically prepared two to three months of homework at a time.

A second approach to developing mixed practice work is to use the process I just described on computer. Use a spreadsheet program and type a set of twelve problems of varying types. Some of the math symbols can be generated by computer, some will need to be written in after printing.

Print the first copy and then use the "search and replace" command to change numbers. For example, tell the computer to replace all "2's" with "3's." Instantly you will see a new set of numbers on the worksheet. Print this out. Repeat this process ten to twenty times and you will generate ten to twenty mixed practice worksheets.

The benefit of using the computer is you can do a cut and paste; that is, bring in a graph from clip art or use geometric figures from other programs.

You can perform similar tricks with a scanner and a printed mixed practice sheet from a textbook. Scan the page and do search and replace commands to create new worksheets. While all of this may sound obscure and unattainable, it is very much within the reach of any teacher who is willing to take a chance and try something new.

Another way to create universal mixed practice is use your math text as a homework component rather than a teaching tool. In class, consider writing problems on the board or on a transparency. When introducing a new concept, don't have students use the text at all. Create problems, in class, as you go. Have students copy from the board rather than the book.

My experience is that when students have a set of problems in a book, as soon as they think they know the process, they tune out of the lesson and begin working ahead. My goal is to keep the students listening to me. When I write problems on the board, I can control the pace, and students are unable to work ahead. This eliminates that familiar refrain of, "What do we do when we're finished?"

When you use your book to assign homework, don't simply assign one page. This does not give students the mixed practice or change of operation they need. Have the students do problem one on twelve different pages. The next night have them do problem two on the same set of pages. A sample assignment might look like: "Do problem one on pages 5, 7, 11, 13, 15, 17, 21, 23, 25, 27, 29, and 30."

If students have difficulty with any problems, the explanation is on that page of the text. The next night, students might do the same pages but this time do problem 3 or problem 10 on each page.

The fourth method one can use to create mixed practice is to purchase materials from a book publisher. I find this to be the least satisfactory because a publisher does not know what you have and have not taught in class. I find it very difficult to find published material which is specific to my

needs. I prefer using a blend of the three methods described on the preceding pages.

On this sample homework assignment sheet, the blue, yellow, and green papers are those created by adding signs

Math Homework

October 18 - November 12

Monday	Tuesday	Wednesday	Thursday	Friday
October 18 Problem 1 on pages: 5, 7, 11, 13, 15, 17, 21, 23, 25, 27, 29, and 31	October 19 Complete Blue Homework Sheet	October 20 Complete Yellow Homework Sheet	October 21 Problem 6 on pages: 5, 7, 11, 13, 15, 17, 21, 23, 25, 27, 29, and 31	October 22 Complete Green Homework Sheet
October 25 Problem 10 on pages: 5, 7, 11, 13, 15, 17, 21, 23, 25, 27, 29, and 31	October 26 Complete Blue Homework Sheet	October 27 Complete Yellow Homework Sheet	October 28 Problem 12 on pages: 5, 7, 11, 13, 15, 17, 21, 23, 25, 27, 29, and 31	October 29 Complete Green Homework Sheet
November 1 Problem 14 on pages: 5, 7, 11, 13, 15, 17, 21, 23, 25, 27, 29, and 31	November 2 Complete Blue Homework Sheet	November 3 Complete Yellow Homework Sheet	November 4 Problem 15 on pages: 5, 7, 11, 13, 15, 17, 21, 23, 25, 27, 29, and 31	November 5 Complete Green Homework Sheet
November 8 Problem 20 on pages: 5, 7, 11, 13, 15, 17, 21, 23, 25, 27, 29, and 31	November 9 Complete Blue Homework Sheet	November 10 Do Chapter Review Test Pages 56 & 57 in math book	November 11 Do Unit review sheet from class to study for tomorrow's test	November 12 UNIT TWO TEST

and doing a search and replace on the computer. I like to use different colors of paper to avoid confusion. The papers can be distributed each day in class or can be given to students for a week at a time in a homework packet.

The concept of Universal Homework as presented in this chapter is unique and perhaps controversial. Over the twenty-seven years that I have been in education, I find I use this approach more and more exclusively every year. Homework is practice; it is important that students complete it, but our instructional time should not be diminished by spending hours every day in bookkeeping and tracking homework assignments.

Universal homework keeps it simple, organized, structured, and professional. I believe it is one of the great time savers that can be implemented by every teacher.

The Year-long Plan
Part Two

With at least a basic understanding of how universal homework is created, we can now finish a year-long teaching plan. The steps of outlining content for each subject area, writing these on a grid, and designing writing assignments were described in the second chapter. Now we bring all of these parts together.

The ideal is to create the month-long homework sheet and from this, do your day-to-day planning. It may seem like a "cart before the horse" approach, but your tests and due dates will appear on the monthly planner. Your challenge as a teacher is to stay on schedule.

When you do monthly planning for the first time, your basic decision is how much homework do you want students to do each night? The homework requirement for first grade will obviously be far less than for a high school class. Is twenty minutes sufficient, or is one hour more realistic?

Also clarify to students and parents that work not completed in class is homework. The twenty to sixty minutes of work which appears on the monthly planner is above and beyond unfinished classwork.

Having used this approach for many years, I have found that when I am as organized as this forces me to be, students also have a tendency to be more organized and more efficient with the use of their time.

The following pages present a monthly assignment sheet for the first month of school. Repetitive aspects are quite noticeable, and this is the point of universal homework. It frees the teacher from tedious hours of planning nightly assignments, thus providing time to do the creative tasks of lesson planning.

The calendar presented on pages seventy-five and seventy-six will remain very similar from one month to the next. Page numbers will need updating. The ebb and flow of tests in social studies, science, and math will need to be scheduled. Assignments in reading will need to be adjusted depending upon the students' pace. Nevertheless, the overall plan for the year can remain intact.

I have used two pages to present each monthly calendar; however, I suggest placing this on one page when given to students. I use the format to make the calendar more readable on the undersized pages of this book.

On the back of each month's calendar, include spelling words, vocabulary for each content area, items in grammar and essential questions in science and social studies. Some of these are provided as an example.

For this sample fifth grade calendar, I chose to limit homework to fifty minutes each night. Students will do math homework Monday through Thursday, spelling three times per week, complete reading from class every night, work on an ongoing writing assignment every evening, and science and

Homework Assignment Sheet

September 13 - October 10

Monday	Tuesday	Wednesday	Thursday	Friday
Sep 13	**Sep 14**	**Sep 15**	**Sep 16**	**Sep 17**
Math: Do problem 1 Pgs. 5, 7, 11, 13,15,17, 21, 23,25, 25,27, 29, 31	**Math:** Complete Blue Homework Sheet	**Math:** Complete Yellow Homework Sheet	**Math:** Do problem 5 Pgs. 5, 7, 11, 13,15,17, 21, 23,25, 25,27, 29, 31	**Writing:** Rewrite opening and closing paragraphs
Spelling: Do activity 1, 2, or 3	**Spelling:** Do activity 5	**Spelling:** Do one activity	**Spelling:** Do one activity	**Reading:** Do two vocabulary activities
Writing: Write opening paragraph	**Writing:** Write closing paragraph	**Writing:** Write one body paragraph	**Writing:** Write one body paragraph	Read Chapter 7
Reading: Finish reading Chapter 3 do one idea	**Reading:** Finish reading Chapter 4 do one idea	**Reading:** Finish reading Chapter 5 quiz tomorrow	**Reading:** Finish reading Chapter 6 do one idea	
Social Studies: Reread pages 16 - 24 do one activity	**Science:** Reread pages 10 - 12 do one activity	**Social Studies:** Reread pages 25 - 33 do one activity	**Science:** Reread pages 19 - 21 questions 1 - 3	
Sep 20	**Sep 21**	**Sep 22**	**Sep 23**	**Sep 24**
Math: Do problem 8 Pgs. 5, 7, 11, 13,15,17, 21, 23,25, 25,27, 29, 31	**Math:** Complete Blue Homework Sheet	**Math:** Complete Yellow Homework Sheet	**Math:** Do problem 9 Pgs. 5, 7, 11, 13,15,17, 21, 23,25, 25,27, 29, 31	**Writing:** Autobiography due Monday if you have not already turned it in.
Spelling: Do one activity	**Spelling:** NONE	**Spelling:** Do one activity	**Spelling:** Study for TEST Tomorrow	**Reading:** Read Chapter 11
Writing: Write one body paragraph	**Writing:** Work on Autobiography	**Writing:** Autobiography tomorrow +10	**Writing:** Autobiography tomorrow +5	
Reading: Finish reading Chapter 8 Quiz tomorrow	**Reading:** Finish reading Chapter 9 do one idea	**Reading:** NONE	**Reading:** Finish reading Chapter 10	
Social Studies: Reread pages 35 - 40 do one activity	**Science:** Reread pages 24 - 27 do one activity	**Social Studies:** Reread pages 44 - 50 do one activity	**Science:** Reread pages 31 - 34 questions 1 - 4	

Homework Assignment Sheet

September 13 - October 10

Monday	Tuesday	Wednesday	Thursday	Friday
Sep 27	**Sep 28**	**Sep 29**	**Sep 30**	**Oct 1**
Math: Do problem 11 Pgs. 5, 7, 11, 13,15,17, 21, 23,25, 25,27, 29, 31	**Math:** Complete Blue Homework Sheet	**Math:** Complete Yellow Homework Sheet	**Math:** Do problem 15 Pgs. 5, 7, 11, 13,15,17, 21, 23,25, 25,27, 29, 31	**Writing:** Rewrite opening and closing paragraphs
Spelling: Do activity 1, 2, or 3	**Spelling:** Do activity 5	**Spelling:** Do one activity	**Spelling:** Do one activity	**Reading:** Finish reading The Lion, Witch & Wardrobe
Writing: Write opening paragraph	**Writing:** Write closing paragraph	**Writing:** Write one body paragraph	**Writing:** Write one body paragraph	
Reading: Finish reading Chapter 12 do one idea	**Reading:** Finish reading Chapter 13 do one idea	**Reading:** Finish reading Chapter 14	**Reading:** Finish reading Chapter 15 do one idea	TEST TUESDAY
Social Studies: Reread pages 55 -62 do one activity	**Science:** Reread pages 39 - 42 do one activity	**Social Studies:** Reread pages 63 - 68 do one activity	**Science:** Reread pages 46 - 49 questions 1 - 3	
Oct 4	**Oct 5**	**Oct 6**	**Oct 7**	**Oct 8**
Math: Do problem 16 Pgs. 5, 7, 11, 13,15,17, 21, 23,25, 25,27, 29, 31	**Math:** Complete Blue - Homework Sheet	**Math:** Complete Yellow Homework Sheet	**Math:** Do problem 17 Pgs. 5, 7, 11, 13,15,17, 21, 23,25, 25,27, 29, 31	**Writing:** Biography due Monday if you have not already turned it in.
Spelling: Do one activity	**Spelling:** NONE	**Spelling:** Do one activity	**Spelling:** Study for TEST Tomorrow	**Reading:** Finish reading Short Story
Writing: Write one body paragraph	**Writing:** Work on Biography	**Writing:** Biography tomorrow +10	**Writing:** Biography tomorrow +5	**Social Studies:** Do two activities for social studies vocabulary
Reading: STUDY FOR TEST	**Reading:** NONE	**Reading:** NONE	**Reading:** Short Story pgs pgs 45 - 56	
Social Studies: Reread pages 72 - 77 do one activity	**Science:** Reread pages 52 - 55 do one activity	**Social Studies:** Answer chapter check-up questions	**Science:** Reread pages 59 - 61 questions 1 - 4	

Homework Assignment Sheet
September 13 - October 10

Spelling words
Weeks 1 & 2

copied	stayed	replied	carried
played	enjoyed	copying	staying
replying	carrying	playing	enjoyed

Weeks 3 & 4

aren't	who'd	doesn't	what's
wood	would	sum	some
garden	season	sometimes	typewriter
whenever	toothache	plow	petal

Social Studies Vocabulary

culture	descendent	ethnic	custom
immigrant	pluralism	predjudice	cartographer
fault	geography	hemisphere	latitude
longitude	meridian	parallel	physical map
projection	region	archives	artifact
chronology	empathy	evidence	historian
interpret	journal	oral history	primary source

Science Vocabulary

biosphere	Earth	hydrosphere	system
atmosphere	interaction	diversity	energy
plankton	lithosphere	meteorites	Mercury
Venus	Mars	rotation	Pluto
Jupiter	Saturn	Neptune	revolution
axis	mass	ellipse	meteor
gravity	solar eclipse		

Reading Vocabulary

air-raid	wretched	courtyard	strategem
alighted	perched	blinking	cramped
wardrobe	flurry	whimpering	alliance
nosing	stoop	vanishing	scheme
kettle	jeering	harness	eternal

77

social studies twice per week. I want to keep each of these assignments to a ten (maximum fifteen) minute block of time.

I encourage students and parents to plan ahead. If families have weekend or week-night obligations, a monthly homework calendar allows the child to complete necessary work in advance. If a student is absent for an extended period of time, he or she can complete the majority of required homework without the teacher's intervention. All of this is effective in terms of our assuming the role of a teacher rather than a bookkeeper.

Adjustments can be made in the quantity of work completed by students with special needs and language difficulties. The organization and structure of month-long planning provides opportunities to make these special considerations.

Year-long planning helps to establish the proper balance between your professional and personal life. The application of this approach is liberating for most teachers. Take the time to plan, and you will find that you have much more time to enjoy.

Opening School

Ah yes, the first day of school — there is something about that first morning that is exciting every year. The kids arrive with their new clothes, new supplies, and in many cases, a new attitude. And regardless of how long we have been teaching, for us it is always sort of a new beginning.

From a time management standpoint, the opening of school is the most important time of the year. It is when we set the tone not only for our students but for our students' parents, our peers, and for ourselves. There are two essential components to starting the year off right and a number of other minor ingredients that will set the stage for the rest of the school year.

The Opening of School Letter

The first correspondence your students' parents receive from you is your opportunity to demonstrate that you are a caring professional deserving of their trust. The more effectively you establish this perception, the fewer problems and

intrusions you will have from them. In your opening of school letter, you want to firmly establish certain aspects of your teaching philosophy and gently present others.

A sample of an opening school letter is provided on the next page. You will notice that it is quite long and covers many topics. Your challenge is to get this letter to your parents before they receive any other correspondence from school. In my case, since I do not receive my class lists until Friday before the opening of school, I write, duplicate, stamp, and seal my letters in envelopes a week or two before school opens. As soon I receive my class lists, I am able to make labels in the school office. If this were not an option, I would spend time self-addressing envelopes to get them mailed Friday morning. Most of my parents receive my letter on Saturday.

The reason I urge you to mail letters early is that on the opening day of school, parents are typically inundated with information. The opening of school message, calendar, free lunch information, sexual harassment policy, walking field trip permission slips, etc. typically go home the first day. If your school does this differently, adjust your schedule so if at all possible, your parents get your letter before their children arrive at school the first day.

Another option is to call each parent the weekend prior to the start of classes. You will not be able to cover all of the topics included in your letter, but you will take a giant step forward in establishing a rapport and sense of respect.

Most teachers will have a Back to School Night scheduled during the second or third week of school. This is the very reason we want to get letters in parents' hands early; waiting for two or three weeks to sell yourself to your parents for the first time is too long.

The most important ingredient to convey in the opening of school letter itself is a sense of professionalism. As mentioned before, any concepts which will be controversial should be described very briefly; but procedures which parents expect to hear — such as your discipline plan, student expectations, homework, and parents involvement policies should be very clearly and forcefully explained.

An important point to consider is that parents need to hear new ideas three times before they believe or understand. For example, if you want to retain a child in kindergarten or first grade, and the first time you present this to parents is at the close of the school year, you will find that these parents will not be particularly understanding or willing to consider this option. If, however, you had met with the same parents in November and casually mentioned retention as an option, met again with the parents in February and were a bit more forceful as retention as a positive option, by the time your May conference surfaced, these parents would have heard the idea three times. Your chances of gaining their support is far more probable.

Using this same philosophy, if you send an opening of school letter and reiterate the information at Back to School Night, by the time parents arrive at the November conference, they will be hearing your policy for the third time. Your chances of gaining their support are far better. This is a realistic approach that makes sense.

Dear Parents:

Once again, summer draws to an end, and it is my pleasure to welcome you and your son or daughter to the eighth grade. In an effort to make this year as beneficial as possible, I want to let you know what to expect in writing with Mr. Purdy this year.

I will be teaching three writing classes and three Spanish classes. Ms. Delavan will work with all seventh grade writing students, and I have all eighth graders.

The organization of the class will be similar to my program of past years. Students will receive a four week gold sheet. Each gold sheet will describe the two writing assignments for that period. In these writing assignments, students will continually be presented with different types of challenges. Some organizational styles we will cover are cause and effect, comparison/contrast, chronology, autobiography and biography, narrative, evaluation, letter writing, interpretation, and description. We will do an extended unit on physical disabilities beginning in January. This unit has been very popular with students in the past.

In addition to writing, students will also work on word derivations, vocabulary development, spelling, grammar (focusing on parts of speech, phrases, and clauses), handwriting, and punctuation.

Students will use a spiral notebook for a variety of creative writing projects, listing rules to be memorized, and daily practice. I will provide this notebook for them. They will not be allowed to take this notebook home until the end of the year. At that point, the notebook will provide a rich resource when they write papers in high school.

My discipline program is simple. My goal last year was to never issue a blue report — I did give one. Needless to say, if your son or daughter receives a blue report from me, a conference is urgent. I will phone parents from time to time, but my emphasis is on making students personally responsible for their work and their success in my classroom. My three classroom rules are:

1. Show respect for yourself and others.
2. Use no off-color language or innuendo in speech or writing.
3. Come to class ready to work, ready to listen, and ready to learn.

Should you have questions about the class, please call or set up an appointment to meet with me. Please avoid "drop-in" conferences as this makes it very difficult for me to prepare and do a thorough job of discussing the situation. My office hours are Tuesday from 3:00 - 4:00 and Thursdays from 3:30 - 4:00.

I will distribute a grade sheet every three weeks so students know where they stand. I will ask that students have parents sign these grade sheets.

I use cassette tapes extensively in my teaching. I find it is a way to "talk" directly to students when I cannot meet directly with them. If you do not have a cassette player at home, this would be an excellent birthday or holiday present. As per school policy, tape players should not come to school with your son or daughter.

When you are curious as to what needs to be done for homework In writing, your two questions should be, "Where's your gold sheet?" and, "If you don't understand the assignment, why didn't you ask Mr. Purdy for a tape?"

I am always willing to provide extra help for students. Typically, the best time to ask for help is after school, but I cannot always assure that I will be available due to meetings, etc. If students ask for help, I will find a time to help them.

Solvang School will continue with its program for classroom donations. Last year, I did not make ongoing requests of parents for these funds. I have purchased 500 cassette tapes, labels, and steno pads (for Spanish), spiral notebooks for creative writing, and will be purchasing a variety of art materials for the students' science projects which we will do this year. Any financial assistance you might provide would be greatly appreciated.

There are some unique approaches I use in my teaching. The procedures I use are based upon educational research and

personal experience. For example, I do not give make-up tests; the next test will count double. There is no extra credit available in my class; however, students may gain "bonus" points for turning assignments in early. Students will also have fewer grades in my class; assignments will be corrected but will not necessarily be graded until I feel students have mastered a specific concept. All graded assignments will receive points for neatness as well as content. I believe we do a disservice to students when accept work that is less than a student's best.

I will more thoroughly explain these procedures at Back to School Night and in addition, will discuss textbooks, use of computers, the role of substitute teachers, and high school preparation.

I am looking forward to another excellent school year. This group of eighth graders is exceptional in their academic ability; I assure you that I will do my best to keep them challenged. I look forward to working with you and with them to make this an outstanding year.

Yours truly,

Scott Purdy

Back to School Night

When your parents arrive at Back to School Night, you should have a second letter prepared for them. It will be similar to your opening of school letter but will emphasize (or sell) some of the more controversial aspects of your program.

In my case, I spend much of Back to School Night explaining why I allow no make-up tests (the next test counts

double in my classroom), why I give fewer grades, why absences in my class are especially detrimental, why I allow no extra credit, and why I cannot possibly read everything that students write. (If you are surprised by some of these approaches, the philosophy of each is explained in other chapters of this book or in my first book, <u>Time Management for Teachers</u>.)

Everything I write in my Back to School Night letter will be explained in class that night; however, many parents do not attend, and many parents have to be in two classes at the same time (two or more children in the same school), and I want both the mother and father to hear from me. My experience is that if one parent comes to my class, all of the information is rarely accurately transferred to the spouse.

I have heard from teachers who have Back to School Night scheduled for the first day of school. In some ways, this is a terrific idea.

For many years I have preached the philosophy that if you are a first year teacher, a teacher new to your grade level, a teacher new to the school, or a kindergarten/first grade teacher, you should schedule a parent meeting on the afternoon or evening of the first day of school. When you alert parents to this meeting prior to the opening of school, you take great pressure off yourself and appease the concerns of many parents.

Remember that parents are sending their most important possession to a completely unknown person for six hours per day. By offering to meet with them the first day, you are recognizing and alleviating their fears. You will also save yourself many one-to-one conferences with curious parents. Primary teachers know what I am describing here.

Other teachers have shared that their schools do not have Back to School Night, and their first opportunity to meet with parents is the first conference time — usually after report cards have been distributed. If I were teaching at a school that did not have a scheduled Back to School Night, I would schedule my own. I find that the second week of school is an ideal time. You are far enough into your program to describe some of your groupings and approaches, yet not so familiar with individual students that you can discuss specific abilities. This stops parents who want to corner you to discuss the progress of their child.

Given this, a Back to School Night on the first day of classes is not such a bad idea. It gives every teacher an opportunity to meet with all parents very early in the year, and since students have only been in attendance for seven or eight days, there is no discussion as to how their child is doing.

There are a few more specific techniques I use at Back to School Night which help to assure the evening will be successful.

The day before the event, send a brief announcement to parents explaining exactly when you will begin your presentation. A sample might be:

Dear Parents of Mr. Purdy's Students:

I wanted to remind you once again that Back to School Night will be held tomorrow night, Thursday, September 15. My presentation is scheduled for 7:30 until 8:00. Since I know several of you will be coming from other classes, I will begin speaking at 7:33 and will finish at 8:00 sharp.

I look forward to meeting with you as I have a lot of information to share about the inner working of our class. I hope you will be able to attend.

Yours truly,

Scott Purdy

The starting time of 7:33 has a purpose. You need to begin training your parents early that your classroom runs in a punctual and orderly manner. If you begin promptly at 7:33, there will be a few minor jokes or comments, but you will also find that parents appreciate not sitting around until 7:40 waiting for others to arrive and then your having to shorten your presentation. You will also be sending the message that at conference times and at other meetings with parents you are "time conscious." Modeling this punctuality will serve you well throughout the year.

Although you have written a letter to parents about Back to School Night, you do not want to let them know this until your presentation is complete. At that point, explain your letter and distribute it to all who want a copy. Also get ten to fifteen envelopes sealed and ready to mail with the Back to School Night letter enclosed.

Offer your students some type of bonus point reward if their parents come to Back to School Night. It does not have to be much, but providing an incentive to assure that your notices get home is a good idea.

When parents come to school that night, write all of your students' names on the white board or chalkboard in the back of the room. On the front board write a note, "Please erase your child's name on the back board so he or she will receive

bonus points for your attendance tonight." At the end of your presentation, remind parents to erase names. On the envelopes you have prepared, write the names of students whose names remain on the board.. The next day in class, have those students address their envelopes or use some of your pre-printed mailing labels. You want every parent to receive your Back to School Night letter.

Before you begin your presentation, write a brief outline of the topics you will cover on the front board. You need not provide an agenda for parents. There is a purpose to writing these topics on the board. Since you only have twenty-seven minutes to speak, you must stay on topic. As soon as a parent asks a pointed question or makes a comment in hopes of putting you on the spot, you can casually turn, point to the board, and say, "I would be happy to answer your question after we finish with the agenda, but I promised that you would be out at 8:00, and I just don't have time to answer your question right now. Please stay after a few minutes and I will speak to you about your concern."

This approach will eliminate parents jumping on a bandwagon or teaming up to put you on the spot. You have been open and honest with them. Don't make excuses for not answering. Proceed with the agenda that is posted on the board.

End on time! Even if you have not covered all topics, finish your presentation in the allotted time. The topics you have not covered will be presented in the letter you provided. It is a good idea to put the most important topics first on your posted agenda. In my situation, the most important items are those which I softly described in my opening of school letter — make-up tests, fewer grades, etc.

To: Parents of Mr. Purdy's writing students

From: Scott Purdy

Re: Back to School Night information

Homework and Writing Assignments: Students will write an extended essay every two weeks. Essays are always due every other Monday; however, students are encouraged to hand in essays on the preceding Thursday for 10 bonus points or the preceding Friday for five bonus points. There will be homework every Monday through Thursday, and all homework is listed on the gold sheet (monthly assignment sheet).

Absences: There is a very strong correlation between number of absences and level of grade. Students do very few worksheets and seat work during class time. I am in front of the class, teaching, 95% of the time. Students learn well from this interactive approach of questioning. My goal is to call on every student at least three times each class period. When your son or daughter is absent, there is generally no work that can be made up. He or she has simply missed fifty minutes of instruction. My homework assignments are structured so that generally, even though a student may have been absent, he or she can usually complete the homework assignment.

Grading: I grade fewer papers than most teachers; however, I, or we as a class, will correct almost all of the work students do. Educational studies indicate that a typical student needs to hear and practice a skill or objective six or seven times before mastery is achieved. I see no point in grading any paper until I have presented information numerous times. I make an important distinction between grading and correcting. Much of what we do in class each day is practice. If students practice thoroughly and with purpose, their grades on writing assignments

89

and tests will improve. One item which I must make clear: If your students are going to write as much as they need to write, there is no way that I have time to read it all. Much of the in-class writing they do will be for practice. I will scrutinize every two week writing assignment. I suggest that you ask your son or daughter to share their work with you before turning it in and after it has been graded.

Tests: Students will take tests every four to five weeks in writing class. All test dates will be listed on the gold sheet. Please try to avoid scheduling appointments or pulling your son or daughter out on a test date. To simplify this, I will generally schedule tests for Wednesday or Thursday. When a student misses a test in my class, there will be no opportunity to take a make-up test. The next test will count double. There are two basic reasons for this. First, it is to any student's advantage to be absent on a test date. He or she has more time to study and will inevitably hear some of the questions from classmates. That makes it unfair for the students who were present to take the test. Second, I want to return tests to students as quickly as possible after they have finished the test. Obviously, I cannot return tests if other students have to take a make-up test. If I wait too long to return the test, any learning that may be achieved from reviewing test results is lost with the passage of time.

Conferences and Office Hours: I will send a grade sheet home with your son or daughter every three weeks. I ask that you review the grade sheet and sign. Students will receive two bonus points if the grade sheet is returned the next day. If you have questions or concerns, please feel free to set up a confer-ence with me. As mentioned in my opening of school letter, my office hours are Tuesday from 3:00 - 4:00 and Thursday from 3:30 - 4:00. If you would like to set up a conference to talk about your son or daughter, please call or send a note. If you can give me a bit of information about specific concerns ahead of time, I will be certain to gather appropriate information. A good conference can

never be conducted on a drop-in basis. I need time to prepare grade sheets, sample work, or to observe behavior regarding a specific concern.

Work Habits and Cooperation Grades: I generally assume that every student entering my room has satisfactory work habits. To me, satisfactory means appropriate. From this base level, students who go above and beyond, who help fellow classmates, who hand in work early, who behave in an exemplary manner, and who show and eagerness and respect for the subject will receive E (excellent) marks. Those who do not exhibit an acceptable level of these behaviors will move down to the U or unsatisfactory level.

Bonus Points and Extra Credit: I do not accept any extra credit in my class; however students can gain bonus points. Students who wish to add extra points to their average may do so in three ways. First, students may turn in written assignments early for ten or five bonus points (as described above). Second, students may earn extra points in class through games, outstanding behavior, and in returning signed forms from parents in a timely manner. Third, students may earn five points whenever a substitute teacher is present. I use this approach because I find many students do mediocre work and at report card time, panic, and want an instant recovery. I prefer to have students budget their time and plan ahead to turn assignments in early. Extra credit rewards students who have been inattentive to responsibilities; bonus points reward students who are thorough and consciencious.

My Personal Philosophy: My writing class is demanding; however, if you speak to former students, I believe you will also hear the comments that it was fun, interesting, and most importantly, students will say that they really learned how to write. Not every student can earn an A, but any student who works hard, completes work on time, seeks help when necessary, and

comes to class every day can earn an A or B. Learning to write effectively is, I believe, the most important skill students learn in school. I want to be remembered as the teacher who taught your son or daughter to write well.

General Opening of School Considerations

Any correspondence which you send home to parents should be pre-approved by your administrator. It is a great idea to have him or her co-sign or at least initial your letters. This sends a subtle message to parents. It also protects you from being undermined by an administrator who does not agree with your philosophy.

From the principal's point of view, a pre-approval avoids him or her being blind-sided by an irate parent. You will make points with your administrator if you obtain pre-approval. This is all part of the "two for ten" concept which is fundamental to time management. Two minutes of time up front, gaining agreement and understanding between you and your administrator, will save ten minutes of turmoil and mis-understanding after the fact.

The first day of school is the time to begin training your students that it is not "your" room (the teacher), it is "our" room (the teacher and students). Your job chart (described in Time Management for Teachers), should be posted and beginning with day one, students should be held accountable for keeping the room neat and clean. Keep in mind that if thirty students each do one minute of cleaning, thirty minutes of cleaning will be accomplished in one minute.

Do not underestimate the power of beginning the school year correctly. It sets a tone for the remaining nine months. As professionals, we must know what we want and must present our policies with assurance and confidence. Your first impression of a doctor, a dentist, or attorney is lasting. You either feel confident in his or her ability or you seek another opinion. In most cases, professionals cannot overcome a negative first impression.

We are professionals! We must demonstrate from day one that we deserve the trust, faith and respect of the students and parents whom we serve.

Twenty-five New Tips

🕐 **Clear Mail Labels**

When we think of mail labels, we usually think of a sheet of white labels. In the past few years, label companies have begun to sell clear labels. In terms of personal use, I always figured that white was good enough for me. However, a few years ago, I was correcting a set of papers, and it seemed that at least ten students made the same type of error. I got tired of writing the same comments over and over and a solution dawned on me — clear labels!

I bought a package of clear return address labels (1/2" by 1 1/4"), did some computer layout and created a page of often-used comments. A reduced version of this page is shown on the next page.

An alternative might be to have rubber stamps made for these comments, but what I especially like about clear labels is I put them on top of student work, in the location in which a mistake was made. The student can read my correction

Comma Rule 1
Use a COMMA after an introductory word, phrase, or clause.
Yes, I believe so
In the past, I was...

Comma Rule 1
Use a COMMA after an introductory word, phrase, or clause.
Yes, I believe so
In the past, I was...

You must always use a comma when you begin sentences with words like "as, since, while, when, because, if"

You must always use a comma when you begin sentences with words like "as, since, while, when, because, if"

Don't begin a sentence with "and" or "but" unless it is used as an introductory clause.

Don't begin a sentence with "and" or "but" unless it is used as an introductory clause.

Don't begin a sentence with "and" or "but" unless it is used as an introductory clause.

Comma Rule 2
Use a COMMA between two descriptive adjectives that can be flip-flopped.
The loud, obnoxious dog
The light brown dog (no COMMA)

Comma Rule 2
Use a COMMA between two descriptive adjectives that can be flip-flopped.
The loud, obnoxious dog
The light brown dog (no COMMA)

Comma Rule 3
Use a COMMA between three or more items in a series – COMMA before "and" is optional.
Jim, Randy and Rene
Jim, Randy and Rene

Comma Rule 3
Use a COMMA between three or more items in a series – COMMA before "and" is optional.
Jim, Randy and Rene
Jim, Randy and Rene

Comma Rule 4
Use a COMMA between two complete sentences joined by and, but, or, nor, for, yet
He went to the party, and he was late. (no COMMA)
He went to the party and was late. (no COMMA)

Comma Rule 4
Use a COMMA between two complete sentences joined by and, but, or, nor, for, yet
He went to the party, and he was late.
He went to the party and was late. (no COMMA)

Comma Rule 4
Use a COMMA between two complete sentences joined by and, but, or, nor, for, yet
He went to the party, and he was late.
He went to the party and was late. (no COMMA)

Comma Rule 5
Use a COMMA to offset unnecessary or parenthetical words, clauses, or phrases: appositives; or words in direct address.
She, to be sure, was surprised

Comma Rule 5
Use a COMMA to offset unnecessary or parenthetical words, clauses, or phrases: appositives; or words in direct address.
She, to be sure, was surprised

Comma Rule 9
Use a COMMA to begin and end quotations unless you use a ! or ?
"I hope," she said, "you will join me."
"Why not?" he asked.

Comma Rule 9
Use a COMMA to begin and end quotations unless you use a ! or ?
"I hope," she said, "you will join me."
"Why not?" he asked.

Comma Rule 7
Use a COMMA between dates and years
May 10, 1999

Don't use the word "and" more than one time in any sentence.

Don't use the word "and" more than one time in any sentence.

Don't use the word "and" more than one time in any sentence.

its - it's
it's means it is (ONLY!) Think of the apostrophe as the missing i.
its is a possessive (ownership)
It's too late to fix its broken leg.

its - it's
it's means it is (ONLY!) Think of the apostrophe as the missing i.
its is a possessive (ownership)
It's too late to fix its broken leg.

its - it's
it's means it is (ONLY!) Think of the apostrophe as the missing i.
its is a possessive (ownership)
It's too late to fix its broken leg.

its - it's
it's means it is (ONLY!) Think of the apostrophe as the missing i.
its is a possessive (ownership)
It's too late to fix its broken leg.

loose - lose
loose means not tight (rhymes with noose)
lose means unable to find
His shoes were loose, and he was afraid he would lose one of them.

NOMINATIVE CASE PRONOUN
I, you, he, she, it, we, they, who
always put yourself second – he and I

NOMINATIVE CASE PRONOUN
I, you, he, she, it, we, they, who
always put yourself second – he and I

choose - chose
choose means to select (rhymes with shoes)
chose is past tense of select
Today I choose the same shoes that I chose yesterday.

choose - chose
choose means to select (rhymes with shoes)
chose is past tense of select
Today I choose the same shoes that I chose yesterday.

who's - whose
who's means who is (ONLY!)
whose is a possessive (ownership)
Who's the person whose voice is loud?

who's - whose
who's means who is (ONLY!)
whose is a possessive (ownership)
Who's the person whose voice is loud?

If the owner is singular, add 's after the word (boy's book)
If the owner is plural and ends in s, add ' (boys' books)
If the owner is plural and doesn't end is s, add 's (women's books)

If the owner is singular, add 's after the word (boy's book)
If the owner is plural and ends in s, add ' (boys' books)
If the owner is plural and doesn't end is s, add 's (women's books)

Don't end one sentence and begin the next sentence with the same word or phrase.

Don't end one sentence and begin the next sentence with the same word or phrase.

There are no such words as "alright" and "alot"
Always write
all right and a lot

There are no such words as "alright" and "alot"
Always write
all right and a lot

Don't begin two consecutive sentences with the same word, or words.

Don't repeat a highly descriptive word in the same paragraph.

Don't repeat a highly descriptive word in the same paragraph.

Don't repeat a highly descriptive word in the same paragraph.

already - all ready
already means previously
all ready means completely prepared
He had already made certain they were all ready

brake - break
brake means to stop a car
break means destroy or ruin
If the brake doesn't work, I'll break my neck.

brake - break
brake means to stop a car
break means destroy or ruin
If the brake doesn't work, I'll break my neck.

past - passed
past is noun or preposition meaning "by"
passed is a past tense verb telling an action
In the past I have passed past the door.

past - passed
past is noun or preposition meaning "by"
passed is a past tense verb telling an action
In the past I have passed past the door.

past - passed
past is noun or preposition meaning "by"
passed is a past tense verb telling an action
In the past I have passed past the door.

quiet - quite - quit
quiet means without sound
quite means very or extremely
quit means to stop working
It was quite quiet in the office when I quit.

quiet - quite - quit
quiet means without sound
quite means very or extremely
quit means to stop working
It was quite quiet in the office when I quit.

than - then
than is a comparison
then tells when
It rather go than now.

than - then
than is a comparison
then tells when
It rather go than now.

than - then
than is a comparison
then tells when
It rather go than now.

too - to - two
too means more or less than necessary or "also"
to means toward (say tuh to decide)
two is more than one

too - to - two
too means more or less than necessary or "also"
to means toward (say tuh to decide)
two is more than one

there - their
there is a place (here) or the beginning of a sentence or independent clause
their shows ownership (e-i-e-i-o)
There are students at their desks over there

there - their
there is a place (here) or the beginning of a sentence or independent clause
their shows ownership (e-i-e-i-o)
There are students at their desks over there

threw - through
threw is past tens of throw or toss
through tells where (a preposition)
He threw the ball through the tire.

threw - through
threw is past tens of throw or toss
through tells where (a preposition)
He threw the ball through the tire.

weather - whether
weather is the conditions outside
whether is a choice (whether or not)
The bad weather will help us decide whether or not to go.

weather - whether
weather is the conditions outside
whether is a choice (whether or not)
The bad weather will help us decide whether or not to go.

weather - whether
weather is the conditions outside
whether is a choice (whether or not)
The bad weather will help us decide whether or not to go.

Avoid beginning every sentence with a pure subject. Use ...
examples: since, while, due to, in addition to, according to, one may also, even though, although

Avoid beginning every sentence with a pure subject. Use ...
examples: since, while, due to, in addition to, according to, one may also, even though, although

Avoid overused words:
examples: fun, like, bored, boring, nice, really, good, supposed to,

Avoid overused words:
examples: fun, like, bored, boring, nice, really, good, supposed to,

Avoid overused words:
examples: fun, like, bored, boring, nice, really, good, supposed to,

A transitions must begin a paragraph!
NEVER end a paragraph with a transition word or sentence

A transitions must begin a paragraph!
NEVER end a paragraph with a transition word or sentence

A transitions must begin a paragraph!
NEVER end a paragraph with a transition word or sentence

Don't end one sentence and begin the next sentence with the same word or phrase.

Don't end one sentence and begin the next sentence with the same word or phrase.

Don't end one sentence and begin the next sentence with the same word or phrase.

Don't begin two consecutive sentences with the same word or words.

Don't begin two consecutive sentences with the same word or words.

Don't begin two consecutive sentences with the same word or words.

and can see through the clear label to see his or her original work. This technique has saved hours and hours of my time!

⏰ Avoid Sending Papers Home

Parents of elementary school students are accustomed to receiving packets of schoolwork every day or each week. If we are going to do less correcting, and if we are not going to read every word a student writes, this can be a problem. There are a number of ways to avoid sending too many papers home.

In my first book, I recommended that students use a spiral notebook or composition book that stays in the classroom. Many daily assignments can be completed in these books. Since they don't leave the classroom, this is one way to avoid sending work home.

Another time-saving way to avoid duplicating worksheets and then collecting papers to correct is to provide students with a small whiteboard, chalkboard, or laminated tagboard. The most workable of these alternatives is also the least expensive.

Cut a sheet of 18" by 24" tag board (any size will work) into four equal pieces (9" x 12"). Laminate each page and then bind the four pieces together into a book. They can be stapled, or better yet, plastic spiral bound. Make one of these for each student.

When you do math problems in class, spelling practice, or any other similar activity, have students use a crayon to write answers (a different answer on each page) in their laminated books. Students then hold their answers "up" so you can read them from the front of the room. The crayon wipes off easily with an old sock (students should bring these from home).

This type of approach is solid teaching! Feedback is immediate, and you can adjust your lesson depending upon the demonstrated understanding of your students.

⊕ Redo work in cooperative groups

One activity I use on homework assignments which are sentence based (translations in a foreign language, grammar practice pages, social studies or science complete sentence answers, etc.) is to have students complete a homework assignment individually, check in class for completion, and then count students off into groups of four. For example, if I have 26 students in class, I will begin pointing to each student, saying 1, 2, 3, ...7, 1, 2, 3, ...7.

After I count them off twice (they never remember the first time), I have all of the "one's" raise their hands (there are five of them since I have 26 students), the "two's" raise their hands, etc.

The instructions are to meet with their "number" group and rewrite the homework assignment on one sheet of paper with all four (or five) group members' names. I warn them that I am going to grade very stringently so they all need to provide input. I give them ten to twenty minutes to complete the task and try to be certain that they are all participating.

If I have one or two students who have not completed their homework, they don't get to work with a group, and they use this class time to complete the homework. Their papers are graded in the same strict manner. Usually, they don't do very well, and it is a clever way to make a subtle point.

The benefits of this technique are numerous. If your homework assignment had students writing eight sentences, instead of having 208 (26 x 8) sentences to correct, you will

have 56 (7 groups x 8 sentences) to correct. Your students will have had the advantage of hearing/discussing this information a second time, and you will efficiently deal with your students who didn't do their homework.

⏱ Write ongoing information in notebooks

Quite often teachers provide a list of rules or a method to use to solve a specific type of problem. If you duplicate copies and distribute them to students, usually many students have lost or misplaced these handouts when you want to review the information.

I suggest you have students write these rules or methods in a spiral notebook which is to be left in class. At the beginning of the school year, when I distribute these notebooks to my students, I have them number each page. They then store these notebooks in their mailboxes* (you can collect them as well). If I am going to review comma rules, I ask that all students open to page one and copy the comma rule from the board as I write it. I go over a few examples and have them make a few notes. The next day, I review comma rule number two, and they write it in their notebooks.

I use the same procedure for all of the lists of memorized items, the various ways to create interest in an essay, etc. The beauty of this approach is that in January or May, I have students turn to page one in their notebooks, and there are the comma rules. They cannot lose them because they never take their notebooks home.

In a seventy page notebook, students are only going to fill ten to fifteen pages of essential or memorized information. What happens to the other pages? This is a second major

---

* The mailbox concept is explained in <u>Time Management for Teachers</u>

benefit to this approach. I usually have students write the important information on pages divisible by five (pages 5, 10, 15, 20, etc.). On the other pages, students do a variety of classroom assignments, creative writing, practice paragraphs or dictation sentences which I read to them.

Since these notebooks never go home, I often do not correct all of the work. This eliminates the questions from parents as to why there were twenty sample sentences completed but only five were corrected. Remember the philosophy regarding practice — students need numerous exposures to a concept before the can gain mastery. The notebook is a way to provide practice without having to correct every example.

⊕ Do less grouping

This suggestion may not concern all teachers, but the reality is that as beneficial as it may be to meet with eight students in a small group, there are fifteen to twenty students during this time that receive no instruction at all. Basically, they are "on hold." Grouping is not beneficial to those students who are not receiving directed instruction.

For many years, education professors and administrators have emphasized the importance of individualization and small groups. Primary teachers, in particular, feel bound to use this as their model for instructional delivery.

There is a definite need for grouping. The suggestion here is to lessen the dependency on this approach. Consider the benefits of less grouping:

First, preparation is dramatically reduced. With three reading groups, the teacher works with one group, and fol-

low-up activities must be planned for two others. Since each of the reading groups is at a different level, this necessitates preparing three hours of material for one hour of teaching. There is no way that any teacher can continually prepare stimulating and motivating lessons in this quantity. Add math groups to the mix, and the task is overwhelming.

Even if you cannot break away from constant grouping, keep in mind that in terms of preparing follow-up materials, two groups require fifty percent less planning than three. Students within each group also receive fifty percent more directed teaching time.

Second, discipline problems are greatly reduced. When the teacher is directing the entire class in a lesson, he or she can immediately respond to a student who is off task. Quite often, when a teacher works with a small reading group, a portion of his or her attention is focused upon what everyone else is doing. As teachers, we continually want to assure ourselves that other students are on task. Is it possible to do our best teaching when we do not have one hundred percent focus upon the group sitting before us?

Third, a question which interests me is, do we really do a better job of teaching when we group students? I am not convinced that three or four reading groups as compared to continual instruction to a whole class is any more effective. Students in any grade level demonstrate radically different abilities. To truly meet the appropriate level of each student wouldn't we actually need to form groups of two or three? Obviously, this is impossible because there are not enough hours in the day. Similarly, I believe there is insufficient teaching time to justify groups of eight or ten. We simply cannot provide enough instructional time with each student if the majority of the day is spent teaching small groups.

Fourth, when we group students, we often spend far too much energy on the logistics of movement rather than the quality of instruction. I have viewed classrooms with elaborate systems of color-coded groups eyeing their color-coded schedules. Every fifteen or twenty minutes, the students effectively rotate from point A to B to C, but I sometimes wonder if they are learning anything other than how to move quickly and quietly from one location to the next. Our teaching and planning time should focus upon instruction rather than scheduling.

Numerous counter-arguments could be made regarding the problems with whole-class instruction. There are second-language issues, ability-level concerns, and the question as to whether or not you really can get to know the students as well. If I were to return to the self-contained classroom, eighty to ninety percent of my instructional time would be whole group.

There is no perfect solution in education; however, in speaking with primary and middle grade level teachers who have lessened the number of groups or altered their dependency upon small groups as the primary means of instruction, feedback has been very positive. Teachers feel as though they can cover more curriculum, spend less time worrying about logistics, and enjoy teaching more because discipline problems begin to disappear.

⨀   **The power of the open gradebook, pen, and bell**

I often get the question from teachers, "What do you do about students who don't do their homework?" I typically

have very few students who fall into this category. I think this is due to four factors.

First, students have homework assignments for the month; there is nightly homework, but it generally points toward an essay or story of some kind. If students don't finish an assigned paragraph on a given night, generally they can write two the next night and catch up. Since my daily lessons are not necessarily tied to homework, those few students who haven't completed it do have a bit of leeway.

Second, I don't collect and correct daily homework. We discuss paragraphs in class and other activities may be completed over three or four nights (vocabulary and spelling). If students do a vocabulary activity on Monday, Tuesday, and Wednesday nights, I will usually collect the three assignments on Thursday. This approach eliminates a lot of the daily checking for completion.

Third, students often have a choice of different types of assignments which they can complete. I find that when students have a choice of writing a poem, creating an audio tape, making a crossword puzzle, or making a set of flash cards, some of the drudgery of homework is removed. If they are choosing an activity which holds a bit of interest for them, they are more inclined to complete the task.

Fourth, if all of my students are going to do the same assignments, we will generally take five to ten minutes of class time to format a paper and do one or two samples. In my experience, students are more inclined to finish a paper which has already been started than they are to complete a paper beginning from scratch.

Given these four approaches, I use a technique when I check homework that seems to get the students' attention. Teachers do not realize the power of an open grade book and

a pen in hand. Quite often when a student has not completed a homework assignment, I will give a look of disapproval, a pause of consternation, and move my pen to the grade book. I rarely make a mark, but the student is unaware of this. To the culprit and to his or her classmates, it appears as though a serious event has taken place — a negative mark in the grade book. My memory is good enough that if a student misses several assignments in a row, there are other ramifications such as study hall, detention, or a call home. Generally, however, very few marks go into my grade book regarding homework. The book in front of me and a pen in hand is often a sufficient deterrent.

The bell is a second gimmick or prop that works well for me. I use a simple hotel desk bell. If I want the class to come to order at the beginning of a class period, after a transition between events, or at the end of the class period, to gain attention to make an announcement, I simply ring the bell and sit paused in front of the class nodding individual approval to those students who come to order. Once again, I move the pen down to the grade book to give bonus points (or to "make" more imaginary marks). I never have to say, "Let's quiet down," or any such call to order. The bell is my messenger, and the grade book and pen are my enforcers.

⏰ Use an overhead pen on whiteboard

Sometimes mistakes can foster new ideas. If your classroom is equipped with whiteboards, and if you write sample sentences or problems on the whiteboard, you can save time by switching between an overhead and whiteboard marker.

As a departmentalized teacher, I often write three to five sentences on the board for students to work with as a warm-

up activity. By mistake, I once wrote these sentences with an overhead pen. As students made corrections and I underlined, circled, and drew arrows from one word to the next, I began to erase one of the sentences and was surprised that only my circles, arrows, and underlining disappeared. The sentence remained on the board. The kids were amazed. "How did you do that?" they asked.

Rather than admitting that I had written with the wrong pen, it dawned on me that I no longer needed to rewrite the sentences two or three more times that day. I also discovered that I could erase my whiteboard marker comments, and correct the sentence a second time as a review. Writing with an overhead pen became a fixture.

In math the following year, I would write a number of problems on the board (with an overhead marker), explain a process, erase my explanation, and have students come forward to complete each problem a second time.

Regardless of how often I use this technique, there is still a sense of mystery expressed by the students when I wipe the board clean and the original sentences or problems remain.

To clean the board completely, I use a moist rag, tissue, or premoistened towelettes that come in a container. It takes a little work to remove the overhead marker so I recommend you experiment with this before using it extensively.

A similar idea is to use a second overhead transparency placed over the top of the first. For example, imagine that you have written five sample sentences for students to copy. Their task is to underline, circle, etc. to identify subjects, nouns, direct objects or other items. If you write on the original transparency, you cannot erase the underlines and other correction marks you have made without also erasing the five original sentences. A second clear transparency placed

top of the first will enable you to write and then erase without destroying the original.

☉ Make multiple copies of class lists on various sized mail labels

At the beginning of each school year, most of us are in an organizational frenzy. One method to free up a lot of time is print labels with students' names on several sizes of mail labels.

You may have noticed that in the corner of the box of almost any peel and stick mail labels you buy, there is a number, for example, "Avery 5161" or "same size as Avery 5161." The 5161 label happens to be 1 inch by 4 inches.

On the computer in either Microsoft Word® or Works® or on a Macintosh® in Clarisworks®, I create a database. If you do not know how to do this, ask a fellow teacher or a high school student to explain. Ten minutes of private instruction is equivalent to two hours of reading a manual.

I am going to explain the process I use on my laptop (now five years old and still using Microsoft Windows® 3.1). If I can do this with my old technology, your newer computer will make it even easier.

Type your students' names into the database and save. Open a new word processing file. Click on the labels or envelopes and labels under the "Tools" heading. You will see a listing of the various sizes of Avery label numbers. Click on fields and then select the database file where you saved your students' names. Select the name of the field in which you typed the students' names. Choose the number label you wish to print and then select "Create Label." When you print, your

printer will automatically space the names properly on the label page.

You might wish to change the font style or size to fit the label more appropriately. To do this, highlight the field and then click on the new font and size. Once again, the computer automatically makes the adjustments.

When you have printed the 5161 label, do the same process and select another size. The printer makes that adjustment.

If you experiment with this process you will find that it will take about fifteen minutes to learn how to print one set of labels. The next set and every set thereafter takes about thirty seconds. I do this process at the beginning of the year and print out two or three sets of labels in various sizes. In one twenty minute sitting, I print labels for student mailboxes, spiral notebooks, file folders, storage boxes, and keep several sets in my desk for future use.

⊕ Create a universal seating chart

Most teachers have a seating chart and quite often it is out of date because it is simply too much trouble to create a new one every time you reassign seats, change your room around, or move one or two students for misbehavior. Even if you are up to date with your current seating chart, this idea will save some organizational time.

At the beginning of the year, I print out a list of labels with student names on 1/2" by 1 3/8" labels (Avery 5167) and use a very small font size, perhaps a 5 or 6. I then get a package of small Post It® note pads.

I place the labels on the notes and trim the sides to make the remaining label as thin as possible. These trimmed labels

become the basis of my seating chart. I stick them on a heavy sheet of paper or cardstock. As students enter the room, and I call roll the first day, I place their Post Its in the correct location on the cardstock. I do not draw lines for desks; I just get the spatial orientation right.

When I have all of the Post Its in place, I put the card stock in a plastic sheet protector. I use a whiteboard pen to write on the seating chart and wipe off my comments or notes after I have transcribed them to my grade book. The seating chart is always clean, and if I need to have two students exchange seats, I simply slide the cardstock out of the sheet protector, move the Post Its to the new locations, and slide the chart back in the protector. It is always up to date. When new students enter, I write their names on new Post It notes and add them to the class — in their proper seating location.

Teachers who teach in the elementary grades can create a second chart with student names and using this same technique can always keep an up-to-date list of reading or math group members, the time and destination of students leaving class for remedial or enrichment work, lists of monitors or helpers, or students with incomplete or missing work.

◷ Use the computer as a time-saving tool

Most of us own or have access to a computer; however, I am still amazed that when I do workshops and teacher inservices, a prevailing mood among at least 40% of the audience is that computers are above and beyond them.

In my first book, <u>Time Management for Teachers</u>, I devoted a chapter to use of technology in the classroom. I do not want to repeat information but will suggest a method for learning to use a computer if you lack confidence.

Step one is to forget the computer manual. You will spend hours of your time deciphering and unlocking jargon. The usual result is frustration and an expansion of the "I cannot do it" attitude.

If you want to learn how to use a computer program, pay an instructor. This may be a fellow teacher, a neighbor, or a high school student with the "tech chromosome." While the instruction is progressing, use a tape recorder to record the lesson. If you try to write procedures, they will not make sense two weeks later. If you try to remember the process, you find the instructions forgotten within days. A tape-recorded lesson will enable you to replay the lesson again and again.

In one hour of instruction, you will learn more than in five hours of experimentation or reading a text. The ten to twenty-five dollars per hour you spend will save hundreds of hours of planning and prep time.

I suggest you learn to use a word processor, a grade book program, and a calendar generation program, in that order.

☉ Use paper of different colors

One way to help yourself and your students get organized is by using different colors of paper for different assignments and handouts. I use goldenrod paper for my monthly assignments sheets. My continual comment in class is, "Check the gold sheet."

A fellow teacher uses yellow paper for important handouts in her math class. Students keep these sheets in a specific place in their notebooks, and if they have a question

about a process or procedure, her line is, "Check the yellow pages."

When you administer a test, try using colored paper. It is not necessary to always use the same color, but I find that when I administer a test, it is very easy to monitor who has and who has not finished. My students turn in their test papers when they are complete. I can take a quick glance around the room and spot a student who is talking and still has a colored sheet in front of him. Other students can retrieve work from their notebooks (white paper) and work while their peers complete the test. The colored paper is a great visual clue.

I suggest you not get too specific about one color for this subject another color for another, etc. You want to develop a system that saves time rather than takes time. Keep it simple.

A few years ago I used a different color for different days' homework assignments, but then I found myself out of blue paper and unable to duplicate what I needed without finding more. I realized then that my system was more trouble than it was worth.

A ream of white paper can be purchased at a discount office supply house for $3.50. A ream of green, blue, pink, or yellow can be purchased for about $4.00. It is worth some extra cost. Better yet, have your district order colored paper as part of their yearly paper supply order.

⏲ Avoid catching students cheating

My guess is that this topic might have garnered a sarcastic thought as you read it. The long version here is, punish students who are caught copying or cheating, but do every-

thing in your power to eliminate the possibility that they can cheat.

This does not mean monitor them more closely when they take a test. That would not be effective time management. Making up two forms of a test, duplicating the test on two different colors of paper to emphasize that there are indeed two different tests, making certain students have mastered the "to be tested" information so they know it so well enough that they won't have to cheat, or changing your test giving format to do more oral questioning are a few of the ways to accomplish this objective.

Why do we need to go to this trouble? If you think about it, when you catch a student cheating, you must confront him or her (privately or openly) thus risking your rapport with the student. You then may be questioned about your sense of fairness when other students begin nipping at you with comments like, "Why are picking on Tommy; lots of other students were cheating, too!" You also eliminate the need to meet with irate parents or explain your situation to an administrator.

When you catch a student cheating, the process ends up depleting some of your energy and enthusiasm for teaching. It is worth investing the time to develop tests and assignments which thwart the students' ability to copy from one another.

Worksheets, chapter check-up questions, and math problems are structured so that it is easy to copy. The reality is, students will copy from one another. For this reason, as well as many others explained in various sections of this book, universal homework assignments, continual work on two-week writing assignments, and correcting work in class help to eliminate the need for you to cross-check student work to see if it has been copied.

We need to make it difficult for students to cheat by being smarter and eliminating the opportunity.

⏰ Pre-plan conferences with parents

One of the most difficult times of the year for both first-year teachers and twenty-five year veterans is parent-teacher conference time. The air is rife with anticipation, worry, discomfort, and in some cases, fear.

When parents arrive in your room for a conference, you must imagine that you are a doctor, dentist, banker, or attorney delivering information that only you could possibly know. This is the stance you must assume — you are the expert and the professional.

If you are insincere, unprepared, timid, overbearing, or incompetent, the conference will not go well. You will have lost credibility not only with the parents with whom you are meeting but with every other parent to whom they complain.

The first step in successful conferences is "no surprises." If the child is doing unsatisfactory work, is a behavior problem, uses inappropriate language, or has any other problems, let parents know this before the conference. Write a note, make a phone call, send grade reports to be signed, mention it after school when they are picking up their child, or have the student write a letter explaining the behavior. Do this at least two weeks prior to conference time.

This may seem overwhelming, but there are probably only five to eight children in your classroom who need this special treatment. Another five to eight are model students. The remainder are students whose work is adequate, and this pre-conference contact with parents is most likely unnecessary.

Identify your "problem" parents, and if necessary, cater to them to some degree. Many parents who criticize teachers are basically insecure about the job they are doing as parents and want to blame someone else for their child's imperfections. From day one, work to gain the support and respect of these parents. You can take a cavalier stance and battle them, but you will lose and will expend a tremendous amount of energy in a pointless confrontation.

You do not have to sacrifice your values or philosophy; you simply need to listen, and try to understand where the parent is coming from. Devise a plan which demonstrates your willingness to meet them half-way.

I meet with many parents every year, and at times, what I would really like to say and what I can say are very different. When I evaluate the situation, I realize that at least eighty percent of parents are supportive, realistic, and respectful. The remaining twenty percent tend to be less realistic in their expectations of me and their child. There is one common factor; they all sincerely want the best for their child. In that regard, we are on equal ground, for I, too, want what is best.

There are three or four parents of students in your class who believe their children are so talented that the work you provide for other children is not challenging enough for their sons and daughters. (Sound familiar?)

My first step would be to meet with each set of parents separately and point out that what their child needs is not more work to do, but to do the work he or she is given to a more developed level. Bloom's Taxonomy is a wonderful reference point in this discussion.

If the class were working on a book report dealing with animal stories, explain to the parents that the more adept

students might consider writing an extra set of paragraphs in which they evaluate the emotions of the main character (animal) in humanistic terms. Offer an extra five points per paragraph for additional interpretations.

The effort required of the teacher in this scenario is minimal. The amount of work for the student is substantial. In my experience, three out of the four of these "gifted" students would prefer to do the minimum amount of work. There will be some who do the more sophisticated work. If so, then they should be challenged in future assignments.

The mere fact that as a teacher you say, "I can," as opposed to, "I cannot provide extra work because..." is a dramatic demonstration of meeting these demanding parents halfway.

The secret in dealing with a parental request for special treatment is to figure out a way to provide extra opportunities that do not require a substantial amount of extra planning. For the remedial student, cut the assignment short; for the gifted student, provide bonus point opportunities for higher level applications.

The second step (after no surprises) in conducting successful parent conferences is to always be on the offensive. Never ask the question, "Do you have any concerns?" This is far too open-ended and gives the parent too much leeway in defining the direction of the conference. Begin with, "I'm glad we have some time to discuss you child's progress. He/ she is doing a beautiful job in.... There are two areas which I believe that if we work together, we can really help your son/ daughter to ..."

Before these lines are spoken, take the time, before the conference begins, to note one or two things the student is

doing well. There is nothing more desirable or rewarding to parents than a compliment paid to them about their child. Remember how hard they are working to raise a child who exemplifies their standards and morals, and how few people ever compliment parents on their dedication. Do not let five uninvolved or uncaring parents out of twenty-five hard-working parents allow you to become cynical. Compliment them and their child!

Next, identify one or two ideas which might improve that student's behavior or performance. Remember, you are the professional; you should be the one to identify the specifics which need improvement.

I try to identify one disciplinary and one academic concern in most conferences. This provides a nice balance of understanding the person and the performance.

The third step in a successful conference is to garner parent support for a plan to change the behavior. Your final statement should be something to the effect of, "I think that by your encouraging Tim to volunteer more in class, and my being certain that he has the correct response when he does volunteer, it will help. I also believe that your signing the homework sheet each night will let him know that we are communicating. I really appreciate your support." In other words, you want to reiterate your plan. The parents of your students need the specifics just as the children do.

If you make certain there are no surprises, pre-plan the positive and negative topics to discuss, and gain final agreement on the process you will use, the uncertainty and aggravation of parent conferences will become a thing of the past.

What does all of this have to do with time management? A ten to fifteen minute conference is ample time if you take the offensive. If you allow parents to set the conference agenda, fifteen minutes will pass before you begin to establish goals. Keep it short and to the point. Parents are a key to success for a teacher. Gain their support by always anticipating and being one step ahead of them.

☾ In art projects, think small

Students generally love to create "art." For some teachers, art is an essential part of the curriculum, and for others, it is more like a craft session in which students do something other than the routine of academics. The art I do in class fits somewhere in the middle; however, there is one time saver that I have discovered in teaching art — think small.

My rule of thumb is, whatever size paper you want to use, cut it in half. For most teachers from third grade through high school level, a 3" by 5" or 5" by 7" card is a good size. If you have 12" by 18" construction paper, cut it down to 12" by 9" or better yet, cut it twice to 6" by 9".

When you give a student a full sheet of paper and say, "Here, create!" it is overwhelming. That, however, is not the true purpose of using smaller paper.

If I have seventy-five students who do an art project in my writing classes, I can display seventy-five, 3" by 5" cards. Every student's work goes on display. For an elementary teacher, the work of all twenty-five or thirty students becomes a full bulletin board. We do not have to spend time selecting which is best, whose work has not been displayed before, or be concerned about hurting anyone's feelings.

Another benefit is that when students know their work is going to be displayed, they have a tendency to take the work a bit more seriously.

From a classroom management and maintenance standpoint, it is much easier to store or file small art projects, and when all work is displayed, you do not have random piles of non-displayed art cluttering the room.

One final benefit is that when the product is smaller, more students finish in a shorter amount of time, and you are less inclined to have to return to the lesson to provide time for completion. Those students who do finish more quickly can do a second project or can help others who have not finished.

☼ Give verbal/oral tests or quizzes

Most of us give quizzes or tests. Quizzes usually check students' understanding of concepts in mid-unit or mid-chapter. Many times these quizzes take a long time to correct and generate the same problems as complete tests in terms of what to do when a student is absent.

One method to consider is giving quizzes verbally rather than administering a written test. This technique takes longer, but the benefit is that every student gets to hear and review the information as you test others. My oral testing takes place for about ten minutes per day over three days. This takes care of the problem of absent students.

You will also find that when you test verbally, you will get an instant indication of what procedures or information is not fully understood by the class in general, and which individuals need more of your attention as you proceed through the remainder of the chapter.

There are two methods you can use to test verbally. Call on one student and have him or her respond to a question or a set of questions and give a score immediately (complete the quiz with one contact), or call on various students and keep a running tally until all students have had an equal number of opportunities to respond. I do both simply to keep students attentive to the process.

If you use the first method, consider giving students an opportunity to improve their scores the following day. This keeps them more focused on their classmates' responses.

☺ Know when to stop hitting your head against the wall

This suggestion involves a difficult decision, yet it is one we must make at least once each year. It is not one hundred percent true, but there is probably an eighty percent correlation that the student who misbehaves, does not do his homework or is absent from class twice per week, probably has parents who will not provide the consistent support that you need.

When these parents come in for a conference, their attitude is sincere and the agreements are clear. For example, the parent will agree to check for complete homework each night and initial the homework page. They will promise to buy the child an alarm clock and make him or her responsible for getting up promptly. They agree that there will be some consequence at home, or they will restrict the child's activities if the weekly note sent home from the teacher indicates misbehavior. This is the plan.

Two days later, there is no follow-through, the behavior continues, and when you again meet with the parents, the

response is that the suggested program did not seem to make any difference. With some parents, there is no follow through.

At what point do you cease to make these contacts with parents? My rule of thumb is, three documented contacts with parents with no results or follow through, and I stop hitting my head against the wall. It always feels so good when I stop!

I move into a teacher-student mode. All discussion is between the child and me; the parents are no longer involved. Sitting down with the student, I describe the program (the consequences are different with every student). Basically, I explain that I will do almost anything to help the child become successful as a student and as a person. I make it clear that I care, but, "You (the child) are telling me that you want to be unsuccessful."

If a child makes this choice, and if the parents provide no support at home, we have to accept that sometimes kids fail. At this point, all misbehaviors, incomplete work, and other infractions are documented and given to the principal on a weekly basis. In most cases, do not let the child know that this documentation is taking place.

The challenge is to work hard to get through to the child, but accept the fact that teachers are not a miracle workers and cannot change every child.

We must be willing to walk towards that student, but until the student takes a step in our direction, he or she is saying, "I want to fail." There's very little any teacher can do when a student has made this decision.

⏱ Letters of recommendation

Not all teachers have to write letters of recommendation for our students, but all of us do write these letters for friends and co-workers. High school teachers write many letters regarding scholarships and college admission. Each time we are asked to write a recommendation, it takes time.

At times, it is flattering to think that someone wants you to write about them. Part of our job is to complete these letters, so how can we do this more efficiently?

First, we must make it clear to those who want a letter that they cannot have it appear instantly. If a student or fellow worker needs your recommendation, it is only fair to let them know that it will take at least one week to complete the letter.

Second, it should not be your responsibility to create or decipher the important content of the letter. In the past, I have had students or co-workers hand me a flyer or brochure. They want me to read, decipher, and write a letter appropriate to the criteria. That is too much for anyone to ask.

A person who wants you to take your time to write a letter for them should do the preliminary work. I created a form to give to people if they want me to write a recommendation for them.

Interestingly, I have had students request a letter, and when given the form, I never receive a completed copy. In this case, there is no letter to write.

Given this situation, it seems fair to assume that the student went elsewhere, or that the letter was not very important to begin with. Either way, it one less letter that I must write.

Letter of Recommendation

Background Information

I consider any letters of recommendation to be confidential so I must let you know ahead of time that I will not provide a copy of the letter for you to read. If you want to see this letter before I mail it, I may not be able to write it.

☐   Please check here if you must see this letter before I mail it

Your name: _____   When must this be mailed? _____

Give me at least a week, please.

To whom should this letter be mailed? complete address, please.

_____ _____

_____ _____

_ _____

_____

What is the purpose of this letter? _____

_____

_____

What are three items you believe would be appropriate for me to write about. Please feel free to brag. This is no time to be shy.

1. _____

_____

_____

2. _____

_____

_____

3. _____

_____

_____

What is the idea behind this letter? Are they looking for intelligence, integrity, professionalism, creativity? What do I need to emphasize? In other words, what is the theme?

_____

_____

_____

_____

121

While this may sound self-centered, consider all that has been discussed thus far. The form on the preceding page is not overwhelming. Is it really too much to ask?

If you want someone to write a letter for you, why not complete this form ahead of time and give it to them when making a request? They will appreciate the guidance.

Another approach to writing letters of recommendation is to ask the person requesting the letter to write it himself or herself and give it to you on disk or email it to you. This may sound bizarre, but this procedure occurs often. Small newspapers, magazines, radio, and television often use reviews of movies, books, plays, or music based upon the press release they receive from the performer or agent.

These reviews are not used verbatim — as provided by the author — but are used as a skeleton from which to build a new article or story. When one considers that the person who knows more about the topic than anyone else is the person who made, created, or authored it, doesn't it make sense to get background information from the source?

In several cases, I have asked very busy people to write letters of recommendation for me. There is no way any of these acquaintances had time to accomplish this had I not provided a skeleton letter about the required topic.

Sometimes we ask people for a letter of recommendation, and that person does not express himself well or does not take pride in the presentation. Since letters are often sent directly to a third party, we have no way of knowing about the quality of the writing. If we provide a sample letter expressing what we feel is important, a person who is a weak writer is inclined to use our wordings. From experience, I can testify to the value of this technique.

Time management and personal management make a good case for pre-writing letters for others to use as models. Make it as simple as possible for them, and ask others to make it as simple as possible for you.

① Take ten salary unit credits per year

Teachers have great health benefits, we have long vacations, we have Saturdays and Sundays off, and we do not get paid enough. There are three positives to counter-balance that one huge negative. Very few teachers went into education with the goal of making "big money." Teaching is not a notoriously high-paying job!

We can, however, help ourselves in some ways not available to other occupations. Most school districts have a salary schedule with steps and columns. The steps represent years of service in the district. This is sometimes referred to as the experience increment (some refer to it as another year and still breathing).

Progress in the columns of the salary schedule are based upon taking college units above and beyond graduation or certification.

As a fifteen year administrator, I was always surprised when during negotiations, a group of teachers, in the final stages of a settlement, would argue for a 2.4 percent cost of living adjustment (COLA) rather than accepting the district's offer of 2.2 percent.

For a teacher making $40,000 per year, this difference of two tenths of one percent is eighty dollars per year. I understand that teachers (we) want to make as much as possible, but the irony in these negotiations was that often the teachers most vehemently arguing for an extra .2% were the very

teachers who were not vigorously garnering salary units to move across the columns of the salary schedule.

A fact for new teachers to ponder... If, as a new teacher, you complete ten salary unit credits per year for the first ten years of your career (and if you never take another salary unit), in the course of a twenty year career, you will earn an extra $170,000. That is $160,000 above and beyond the cost of units. It makes .2% ($80) per year seem paltry when compared to an average increase of $8,000 per year by taking salary units.

For a teacher who completes a thirty year career, the extra earning totals $242,000.

These figures are based upon an average cost of $120.00 per semester unit, a salary schedule with a $1,200 increment between each column (eight possible columns), and a COLA of two percent.

A teacher is confronted with salary unit opportunities on almost a daily basis. Graduate schools are eager to take your money so they offer a remarkable array of classes from the fascinating to the pointless; nevertheless, the opportunities abound.

I firmly believe it is possible for a classroom teacher to complete ten semester units of classes in a three month period of time while teaching full time. If you call the state university in your home state and ask for their independent or correspondent studies catalogue, you will be surprised by what is offered. Videotape classes, audiocassette classes, internet classes, Friday night/Saturday classes, and independent study classes; you name it, it is offered.

I find it more and more difficult to attend a nine week course with a meeting every Tuesday (for example). I have difficulty committing to a program this long. But I can take a

four semester unit Spanish 3 courses using audio tapes, a student workbook, and a text. I can complete the entire course in three months and leave my home just one time to take a final exam at a local junior college. I do my studying and class work assignments for fifteen minutes every night before going to bed. No driving and no sitting in class. All it really takes is self-discipline and the initial cost of the course.

I can take a second course (three semester hours) by watching educational programming on public television. A third course (one semester unit) can be completed in a one weekend seminar, and another course can be taken on the internet (two semester units).

Yes, most of us would rather be doing something other than taking classes. However, if we teach for another twenty years, the investment of hours this year will earn an average of an additional $46.00 per day for every day of the 180 day school year we work each year. That is $170,000.

It is worth it to sacrifice some time to take units if we can earn forty-six more dollars every day. We may as well make more for doing the same job.

① Evaluate the importance of office paperwork

As teachers, we have numerous administrative paper-work commitments. I am not including correcting or grading student work here; this concerns the office information, student checklists, and questionnaires.

To complete these quickly, develop a scale with which to rate the importance of any papers which must be returned to the "office." I use a rating scale of one to five.

A five is very important — it has to do with your job security. A one is pointless — it does not make sense and is a

waste of time to complete. Two's, three's, and four's fall in-between in terms of importance.

Accept that every paper must be filled out and returned to the administration as quickly as possible. The decision which one must make is how much time does the completion of the paper warrant? Consider who is making the request, and what the benefit to your students will be.

As a former administrator, I am well aware that much paperwork is generated in people's effort to justify the importance or necessity of their position. If an employee is receiving pay for an administrative task, he or she needs to show something concrete to justify the pay.

I find that in most cases, papers created by a person to justify a job, rate a one or two on my scale. I complete the paper but with minimal effort or thought. Usually, it is not the information that is necessary, it is the completed paper filling a file drawer that is essential. I believe that if that person wants more information, he or she will come and ask for it. This one-to-one meeting is my perfect opportunity to question why we were given the paper in the first place.

Many districts are fascinated with compiling student port-folios or mastery checklists. I always question this approach only because I know very few teachers who ever refer to this information from one year to the next. I also cannot imagine that any administrator has time to look through these indi-vidual student profiles. If your district has created an objec-tive mastery profile that everyone uses, it ranks as a five. In most districts, these profiles are a two or three.

Special education teachers are required to complete a myriad of papers for each student on their caseload. When they ask for information, this is a four or five. If you be-grudge the time spent on these forms, take a moment and be

thankful that they are compiling all the necessary information. Until one has worked in the legal jungle of special education, it is almost impossible to imagine this paperwork nightmare. Be kind and thorough.

There are numerous other papers that magically appear in our mailboxes or on our desks. If you are curious as to why you must complete the form, ask the question. When I seek out the person and ask, the response is often, "Oh, not everyone needs to do that; we just gave one to everyone because we weren't certain who was affected."

Only about one of every five papers that comes from the chain of command is vital. Keep this in mind the next time you spend an hour of your time doing someone else's work.

⏱ The Career Notebook

This is a time saver and keepsake in one package. Each year we have a school picture taken with our students. Teachers usually get a copy for free and for many years, I kept placing them in a file labeled "photographs."

Two years ago I began keeping a photograph book with the class picture on one side, and a sheet of paper on which to write memories on the opposite page. The "lift up" sticky plastic photo album works well. On the paper, I write various lists of assignments which worked particulary well, art projects which students enjoyed, humorous or thought-provoking comments by that year's students, or other items I want to remember in the future.

It takes very little time to make the additions, but in two years, I have begun to build a compendium of ideas and thoughts to refer to as I do year-long planning. I wish I had started this twenty-eight years ago when I first started teach-

ing. We forget so many of the little things that we and our students do. The career scrapbook is a way to keep many memories and teaching ideas in one place.

☺ The New Student Packet

Each year we experience the frustration of having made all of our folders, seating charts, and grade book listings, when all of a sudden, the school secretary stands at the classroom door to introduce us to a new student. We are compassionate and welcome the student to the room, but in the back of our minds we are a bit irritated. The group was working well, they knew the rules, the diagnositcs had been done, and now we begin again.

There are a few time management techniques that can help to minimize the impact of this new student.

First, at the beginning of the year get ten file folders and every time you make copies of papers to hand to your students, make ten extras and place one of them in each file folder. Also include the opening of school letter, Back to School Night information, the opening of school packet from the office, and any other information you usually distribute at the beginning of the school year.

Second, compile a set of diagnostic tests, several stories with comprehension questions from a basal reader, three or four math drill sheets, an encyclopedia article from which the student can write a short synopsis, duplicated copies of the first chapter of the social studies and science books, and some type of proofreading paper in which the student must identify spelling and punctuation errors.

To put it bluntly, this is a "keep 'em busy" packet that will allow you to assess the abilities of the new student with-

out having to place the remainder of your class "on hold." The benefit of compiling this packet of student materials ahead of time is that you only need do it once. One packet goes in each file folder.

Many teachers face an extremely high transiency rate and every time a new student walks into the room, there is a flurry of activity to find all of these materials. We are going to do all of this anyway; why not do it one time and have it completed?

You may consider doing a second packet of materials for those students who are non-English speakers. Of course, it creates more initial work. Then again, how many times have you had some poor soul walk into your classroom and stare blankly at you because he or she had nothing to occupy the time?

🕐 **Library pocket charts**

Many times we need to remind our students of bits and pieces of information. On any given day in the classroom, there may be four students who need to return a form sent to parents, one or two students who were absent who are missing a homework assignment, another two students who have to rewrite a paper, and one class member who has not returned a discipline letter.

It takes a lot of time and effort to get all of these reminders to students. I use a system that provides a consistent reminder to me and to my students. It is very inexpensive to create and the beauty is in its simplicity.

Ask your librarian if he or she has any old book pocket envelopes. These are about four inches by four inches and were glued to the front inside cover of books with a signature

card slipped inside. With bar codes and computerized check-out systems, few librarians still use this old circulation system. Chances are they have a drawer full of old pocket envelopes. If your library does not have these, check the Demco library catalogue or a stationery superstore. You will need one envelope for each student.

Write one student's name on each envelope, and glue them onto a heavy sheet of tagboard or poster paper. Display the chart in the front of the room.

Your next step is to get several different colors of paper and cut several four by one inch strips of each color. The next challenge is to list all of the different reminders you must provide for students, and to match these to different colors with some meaningful (or silly) correlation. My list includes:

• Late assignments (major)	Late lavender
• PTA flyers & fund raising	PTA purple
• Rewrites of work	Rewrite red
• Signed grade sheets	Grade sheet grey
• Parent consent forms	Parent pink
• Library books	Blue books
• Please see me	Black

A primary teacher might add a milk money or meal ticket reminder (this is a convenient way to return meal tickets to students for those schools that use them), homework folders, or a note from home excusing an absence.

To help students remember the color codes, glue extra envelopes on the bottom row of the chart, label them with the corresponding topic, and use these to store the extra color strips.

My goal is to have as few color strips on the chart as possible. I like color-coding rather than writing a note because it provides a reminder from a distance. The goal of the students is to leave the room each day with a clean envelope. When something occurs to me during class, before school, or after students have left for the day, I don't worry about notes, I put that color in the student's envelope.

There are variations to this approach. The envelopes with color strips can be used to guide students to various groups or centers during the day. They can be used to assign specific homework questions to individual students. For example, in physics, geometry, calculus, or chemistry classes, there are often more chapter review questions than can possibly be completed by one student. The teacher might use color-coding to assign specific questions to groups of students.

Another use of these charts is to randomly assign students to cooperative groups. If a teacher has thirty-one students and wants to quickly divide students into groups, he or she can use four strips of eight different colors and randomly place them in envelopes. When students enter the room, they need only be reminded to meet with those students who share their color.

The same approach works for teaming students for in groups of two's, three's, four's, or ten's. Many times when a teacher does this ahead of time, it solves the problem of having students say (or think), "I don't want to work with Jimmy." The decision is made when they walk into the room. In addition, when students have left, the teacher has a record of which student was in each group.

This idea is quick to implement, inexpensive, and most teachers find it saves time.

⊕ Get a cellular phone

I do not happen to be a fan of cellular phones; however, I have spoken with many teachers who do not have a phone in their classroom and find that the convenience of a cell phone is a valuable time saver.

It seems absurd that teachers do not have phones available in the room. After all, administrators stress the importance of keeping parents informed, but if one cannot speak from the privacy of the classroom, how can a candid talk with parents occur? We are professionals with five years of college education; and we are not entrusted with a phone on our desks! I believe every teaching staff in the United States should vote against the purchase new computers until a phone system has been installed in the school.

In the interim, a cell phone can provide availability and convenience at a relatively low cost. I often hear the additional selling point that the phone is tax deductible. This is true, but most teachers I know are not worried about deducting the cost, they are more concerned with finding the money to buy a phone in the first place.

⊕ Create absentee and independent study packets

Often students come to us and ask for "work" while they are going to be away on vacation or family business. They do not necessarily want work, but they (and their parents) do not want to be behind when they return.

From the time I send my opening of school letter, I try to impress upon students and parents that there is no work that can be made up when a student is absent. The homework must be completed (since it is universal), but the work in

class is based upon direct instruction rather than completing worksheets.

When a student is absent for three days or more, I believe it is important to require the student to do something to make up for the class time he or she has missed. Often I record the independent study on a cassette tape, but I also created this simple check-off sheet (see next page) so I can quickly give students extra assignments.

In addition to the requirements that I select for the student to complete, he or she must also do all homework described on the monthly assignment sheet I provide.

Each teacher must decide how to implement his or her independent study policy. It is easy to take the suggested ideas and adapt them to almost any grade level. Grades need not be given on this extra work. The message we must send to students is that even though they are going to be away from school, they must still complete work for school.

The attitude we should adopt as teachers is that it is not our responsibility to provide an education for children whose parents believe it is acceptable to pull their children from school for extended periods of time. I understand the necessity of parents taking vacations when they have the time available. I applaud them for taking their children with them. However, I will not accept that it is my responsibility to provide long-distance instruction given these circumstances.

⊙ **Create a card file folder for ongoing record keeping**

Often it is convenient to keep records of individual students' progress in certain subject areas; for example, in my writing classes, I find it helpful to make a note of specific

133

Independent Study Assignments

Complete all assignments that are checked.

☐   Write a 150 word journal entry for every school day you miss. Explain what interesting things you learned, and describe the interesting place you visited.

☐   Collect three leaves that are different than what you typically see in Santa Barbara County, and find out what type of plants they are.

☐   Interview a person you meet during your vacation, and write a paragraph of at least 100 words which tell why he or she likes/dislikes living in the place where you are vacationing.

☐   Draw four pictures of interesting buildings, scenes, or people you see on your trip. You may draw all four on one sheet of paper or use a different sheet for each scene.

☐   In your absolute best cursive handwriting, copy the saying or explanation that appears on an historical building or monument that you visit. It must be at least 50 words in length.

☐   Make a list of ten people whose names I would recognize who live or lived in one of the places you are visiting.

☐   Write a list of the ten best and the ten worst things that happened during your vacation. I am not looking for personal incidents. I would prefer to hear about your interaction with the people and places.

☐   Write a paragraph of 150 words which explains how the lifestyle and people are different than what you are used to. Include comparisons on language, accents, food, expressions, expense, local interests, and other differences you noticed.

skills I want particular students to focus upon in an upcoming paper. On each extended writing assignment I receive, I make cryptic notes about the progress and goals of each student.

A former student shared an idea of taping index cards in a file folder making the cards easier to carry and more accessible. I found this to be extremely useful. In my departmentalized setting, I use classification folders for this purpose. These are folders with two or three rigid pages within a standard file folder. They are available at any well-stocked stationery store.

To make my "card file folder," I use 5" by 7" index cards. Taking the first card, I place a long piece of cellophane tape along the upper edge of the card. I overhang the tape by half of its width so I can tape the card to the lower portion of the file folder. After positioning the first card, I take the next card, place tape along the upper edge, and position it slightly higher on the inside cover of the file folder. I can fit about fifteen cards on one side of a folder.

The students' names are written in alphabetical order on the exposed lower edge of each card thus allowing immediate access to each student's card. This is a much faster and more portable method than keeping a bundle of cards secured with a rubber band.

Professional Teaching

I love teaching and respect our profession, but I am often disappointed that we (teachers) are our own worst enemy. Too often, we do not present ourselves as professionals.

We have the responsibility and education, but we do not seem to place ourselves on the same level as doctors, CEO's, bankers, and attorneys. When I mention this in my seminars, I always hear a reference to low pay. I find this ironic in that I have never met a teacher who stepped into the classroom for the purpose of acquiring wealth. We knew we would not get rich when we signed up for this job.

Salary does not prevent us from being professionals. In general, it is our attitude and demeanor that are holding us back. We must change our self-perception because if we do not respect ourselves, we will never attain the status we deserve.

In this chapter, I present my personal philosophy and advice. I realized many years ago that I would never change society's opinion of teachers until I, myself, adopted a new attitude. It occurred to me that I could never change everyone, but I could change myself.

I also discovered that as I gained heightened self-respect and respect for my profession, I received more respect from my colleagues, students, and from their parents. I no longer am questioned as to why I do what I do, or why I teach what I teach. I became a professional and an expert in my field. After all, if I do not believe in me, why should anyone else?

Dress as a professional

First impressions are based upon outward appearance. Before we have a chance to open our mouths, we have been judged by our looks. A few years ago, I dropped my son off at school and saw one of his teachers walking into the class-room wearing shorts, a T-shirt, and sandals.

I am certain that I could get away with this casual look. I could still teach and am confident that my students would learn. I choose to wear a tie to work each day, along with a clean pair of slacks, pressed shirt, and polished shoes. I do not have to, but I do because that is the way professionals dress. I expect my doctor, banker, and tax preparer to show me respect by dressing professionally. I believe my students want me to extend this same courtesy to them. I deserve it, and they deserve it.

We do not have to be high fashion, but we need to be high quality.

The wisdom of Thumper

Thumper is a young rabbit in the Disney movie, Bambi. While it has been many years since I saw this movie, I do remember one bit of advice which he provided, "If you can't say something nice, don't say nothin' at all." This is excellent staff room etiquette.

In every school, the tone in a teachers' lounge tells volumes. There are lounges which are so vitriolic that the mood is almost poisonous; there are others which are filled with humor, jokes, and pranks; still others are completely professional and collegial. Veteran teachers who have been at various school sites know how varied the atmosphere can be.

Regardless of the tone in the lounge at your school, you can still be a professional. Do not buy into negativism. You need not be Polyanna or Mary Poppins and talk incessantly about how wonderful everything is. This personality style can be as annoying as the chronic complainer. Simply make up your mind that when you open your mouth, your comments will be positive. If they are not positive or productive, do not open your mouth.

When one thinks about it, what possible good can come from griping about a students' behavior, complaining about lack of support from a parent, an administrative decision made three months prior, or a fellow teacher who irritates you? Every teacher in the world faces these problems. The professional should not broadcast complaints to anyone and everyone who will listen. When we gripe in public, we do ourselves and our profession a great disservice.

If you have a complaint, the best way to handle it is to talk, one-to-one, with a fellow employee whom you respect and trust. Keep in mind, however, no one cares about your problems as much as you do. Venting can make you feel better momentarily, but the problem will continue until you find a solution. Avoid burdening a colleague with constant gripes. He or she only has so much time to listen to you.

One other approach to consider: Do not complain about a problem unless you have a solution. As a teacher, it is not my job to solve the overall problems of the school. That is

twenty percent notice the error and think less of you because of it. As professionals, we cannot afford this reputation.

When you write a letter to parents, spell check and proofing are not enough. You must have a spouse or colleague read the letter and point out awkward wordings or expressions which may be offensive.

As an example as to why another person's opinion is essential, I recently wrote a letter to the parents of students in my class explaining my approach to in-class instruction. I used the expression, "I am continually firing questions at students." My wife, and proofreader, circled the word "firing" and said it sounded intimidating. She was right, and I reworded the section.

My point is that when we write, we may believe we are communicating very clearly. The same words, however, are not perceived identically by everyone. We must get a second opinion before we send these letters home.

Don't give away your expertise

As teachers, we have a professional obligation to serve on curriculum committees, attend special education meetings, and participate in staff meetings and district inservices. Above and beyond job requirements such as those listed, we should be paid for other adjunct responsibilities we assume. There is nothing wrong with asking the question, "Will there be extra compensation?"

School districts spend thousands of dollars on consultants, studies, paraprofessionals, trainers, planners, and repairmen. You are entitled to be paid for your professional expertise. The dentist may come in on a weekend to fix your broken tooth. We view this as an act of kindness, but we still

get billed for it. Bankers charge us for the loans we receive, doctors charge for the lab work we have done, attorneys charge by the minute, and teachers feel as though it is our responsibility to do all of the extras for free.

When we use our expertise to enhance teaching, we should be paid for it. If we are not compensated, let others do the work. When we are paid, we should receive remuneration comparable to other professionals.

I believe it is fair to assume that if we perform a service for our school or our district, we should receive at least $75.00 per hour. If the district is unwilling to pay, let someone else perform the service. It comes down to a matter of supply and demand — if a district will pay what we deserve, we will supply the information.

Be the committee chairperson

Every committee needs a leader, and when you are required to serve on a committee, always volunteer to be the chairperson. When you are in charge, you can set the meeting times to your convenience, decide how long each meeting will last, make the decision as to when your task is complete, delegate others to do the things you do not want to do, and make final decisions to assure the results you most desire.

While this sounds manipulative, it is not. Someone must lead, and if you do not volunteer, someone else will. You will then be bound by his or her decisions. Professionals take charge and achieve results.

Eight out of ten isn't bad!

Too many of us are under the impression that we must please everyone. To be blunt, pleasing everyone is impossible and there is no sense in trying. I firmly believe that at least five percent of our constituents are in a "try not to please" fringe. This means that if you have made the members of this small group happy, you are probably alienating a large number of your supporters.

No one respects a "yes man/woman" for very long, and very few can tolerate an indecisive person. If these are traits in a professional person, he or she will not stay in business very long.

A teacher must make hundreds of decisions every day. We tell children they cannot behave in certain ways and while they may not like constraints, we do it because we know it is in their best interest. Likewise, one or two parents may not like how we do certain things. If we have a logical and educationally sound reason for doing what we do — it does not matter if they do not like it. We are the professional decision makers. It is our job to do what is best for the majority.

Be a teacher first and a teacher second

This redundant heading has a point. Our job is to educate children. We are not trained counselors, psychologists, child therapists, or big brothers and sisters.

Every day in the classroom we perform all of these roles to some degree. We must, however, keep a professional distance from our students. If we are to be role models and

inspirations for greatness, we cannot also be a confidant or a "buddy."

Compassionate, yes. Sympathetic, yes. Interested, yes. A counselor or therapist, no. If you wish to counsel young people, become a counselor. The professional teacher has the responsibility to inspire and to teach.

Your classroom

When a student or parent walks into your classroom you are sending them a message. If your room is organized, clean, and cheerful, they respond accordingly. If piles of paper and catalogues cover every surface, miscellaneous paint, rags, cleaning fluids, and random paper towels fill the sink counter, and you cannot find anything you are looking for, you are sending a very different message.

Would you want to deposit your money at a sloppy or unclean bank? Would you return to a doctor whose examining room had used cotton balls and tongue depressors strewn about the counter surfaces? Would a tax preparer who could not find your file, the company handbook, or a pencil or pen with which to write instill confidence in the work he or she had done for you?

We expect professionals to exhibit a certain sense of cleanliness, order, and control. When a parent walks into a classroom and sees dirt, chaos, and disarray, he or she will never be fully confident that you can do the job of educating his/her son or daughter.

In my first book, there are numerous ideas about keeping your classroom in order. Professional teachers must take pride in every aspect of their workspace.

After reading this chapter, one may wonder how all of these suggestions are related to time management. I believe they are inescapably relevent. People who manage their time eliminate wasted moments.

It is wasteful to spend your time trying to overcome a perception. Your dress, demeanor, speech, surroundings, writing, and commitment are based upon perception. What people perceive is what they believe.

Practicing the suggestions in this chapter will not make every teacher excellent; however, modeling these ideas will make every teacher more professional and efficient. With with efficiency comes the benefit of saving time. And time management is what this book is all about.

9456